200 Light
sugar-free recipes

hamlyn | **all colour cookbook**

200 Light
sugar-free recipes

An Hachette UK Company
www.hachette.co.uk

First published in Great Britain in 2015 by
Hamlyn, a division of Octopus Publishing Group Ltd
Carmelite House
50 Victoria Embankment
London EC4Y 0DZ
www.octopusbooks.co.uk

Recipes in this book have previously appeared in other books
published by Hamlyn.

ISBN 978-0-600-63214-6

A CIP catalogue record for this book is available from the
British Library.

Printed and bound in China

1 2 3 4 5 6 7 8 9 10

Standard level spoon measurements are used in all recipes.
1 tablespoon = one 15 ml spoon
1 teaspoon = one 5 ml spoon

Both imperial and metric measurements have been given in
all recipes. Use one set of measurements only and not a
mixture of both.

Ovens should be preheated to the specific temperature – if using a
fan-assisted oven, follow manufacturer's instructions for adjusting
the time and the temperature.

Eggs should be medium unless otherwise stated. The Department
of Health advises that eggs should not be consumed raw. This book
contains dishes made with raw or lightly cooked eggs. It is prudent
for more vulnerable people such as pregnant and nursing mothers,
invalids, the elderly, babies and young children to avoid uncooked or
lightly cooked dishes made with eggs. Once prepared these dishes
should be kept refrigerated and used promptly.

Milk should be full fat unless otherwise stated.

Fresh herbs should be used unless otherwise stated. If unavailable
use dried herbs as an alternative but halve the quantities stated.

Pepper should be freshly ground black pepper unless
otherwise stated.

This book includes dishes made with nuts and nut derivatives. It
is advisable for customers with known allergic reactions to nuts
and nut derivatives and those who may be potentially vulnerable
to these allergies, such as pregnant and nursing mothers, invalids,
the elderly, babies and children, to avoid dishes made with nuts
and nut oils. It is also prudent to check the labels of pre-prepared
ingredients for the possible inclusion of nut derivatives.

Vegetarians should look for the 'V' symbol on a cheese to ensure it
is made with vegetarian rennet.

contents

introduction

introduction

this series

The Hamlyn All Colour Light Series is a
collection of handy-sized books, each packed
with over 200 healthy recipes on a variety of
topics and cuisines to suit your needs.

The books are designed to help those
people who are trying to lose weight by
offering a range of delicious recipes that are
low in calories but still high in flavour. The
recipes shows the calorie count per portion,
so you will know exactly what you are eating.
These are recipes for real and delicious food,
not ultra-slimming meals, so they will help you
maintain your new, healthier eating plan for
life. They must be used as part of a balanced
diet, with the cakes and sweet dishes eaten
only as an occasional treat.

how to use this book

All the recipes in this book are clearly marked
with the number of calories (kcal) per serving.
The chapters cover different calorie bands:
under 500 calories, under 400 calories, under
300 calories, etc.

There are variations of each recipe at the
bottom of the page – note the calorie count
as they do vary and can sometimes be more
than the original recipe.

The figures assume that you are using lean
meat, so make sure you trim meat of all visible
fat and remove the skin from chicken breasts.
Use moderate amounts of oil and butter for
cooking or low-fat/low-calorie alternatives
(see page 13).

Don't forget to take note of the number
of portions each recipe makes and divide
up the quantity of food accordingly, so that
you know exactly how many calories you are
consuming. Be careful about side dishes
and accompaniments as they will add to the
calorie content.

Above all, enjoy trying out the new flavours
and exciting recipes that this book contains.
Rather than dwelling on the thought that you
are denying yourself your usual unhealthy
snacks and treats, think of your new regime
as a positive step towards a new and
improved you. Not only will you lose weight
and feel more confident, but your health will
benefit, the condition of your hair and nails

will improve, and your skin will take on a healthy glow.

the risks of obesity

Up to half of women and two-thirds of men are overweight or obese in the developed world today. Being overweight not only can make us unhappy with our appearance, but can also lead to serious health problems, including heart disease, high blood pressure and diabetes. When someone is obese, it means they are overweight to the point that it could start to seriously threaten their health. In fact, obesity ranks as a close second to smoking as a possible cause of cancer. Obese women are more likely to have complications during and after pregnancy, and people who are overweight or obese are also more likely to suffer from coronary heart disease, gallstones, osteoarthritis, high blood pressure and type 2 diabetes.

how can I tell if I am overweight?

The best way to tell if you are overweight is to work out your body mass index (BMI). If using metric measurements, divide your weight in kilograms (kg) by your height in metres (m) squared. (For example, if you are 1.7 m tall and weigh 70 kg, the calculation would be 70 ÷ 2.89 = 24.2.) If using imperial measurements, divide your weight in pounds (lb) by your height in inches (in) squared and multiply by 703. Then compare the figure to the list below (these figures apply to healthy adults only).

less than 20	underweight
20–25	healthy
25–30	overweight
Over 30	obese

As we all know by now, one of the major causes of obesity is eating too many calories.

what is a calorie?

Our bodies need energy to stay alive, grow, keep warm and be active. We get the energy we need to survive from the food and drinks we consume – more specifically, from the fat, carbohydrate, protein and alcohol that they contain.

A calorie (cal), as anyone who has ever been on a diet will know, is the unit used

to measure how much energy different foods contain. A calorie can be scientifically defined as the energy required to raise the temperature of 1 gram of water from 14.5°C to 15.5°C. A kilocalorie (kcal) is 1,000 calories and it is, in fact, kilocalories that we usually mean when we talk about the calories in different foods.

Different food types contain different numbers of calories. For example, a gram of carbohydrate (starch or sugar) provides 3.75 kcal, protein provides 4 kcal per gram, fat provides 9 kcal per gram and alcohol provides 7 kcal per gram. So, fat is the most concentrated source of energy – weight for weight, it provides just over twice as many calories as either protein or carbohydrate – with alcohol not far behind. The energy content of a food or drink depends on how many grams of carbohydrate, fat, protein and alcohol are present.

how many calories do we need?

The number of calories we need to consume varies from person to person, but your body weight is a clear indication of whether you are eating the right amount. Body weight is simply determined by the number of calories you are eating compared to the number of calories your body is using to maintain itself and needed for physical activity. If you regularly consume more calories than you use up, you will start to gain weight as extra energy is stored in the body as fat.

Based on our relatively inactive modern-day lifestyles, most nutritionists recommend that women should aim to consume around 2,000 calories (kcal) per day, and men an amount of around 2,500. Of course, the amount of energy required depends on your level of activity: the more active you are, the more energy you need to maintain a stable weight.

a healthier lifestyle

To maintain a healthy body weight, we need to expend as much energy as we consume; to lose weight, energy expenditure must therefore exceed intake of calories. So, exercise is an important tool in the fight to lose weight.

Physical activity doesn't just help us control body weight; it also helps to reduce our appetite and is known to have beneficial

of 10 minutes are equally beneficial. Children and young people should be encouraged to take at least 60 minutes of moderate-intensity exercise every day.

Some activities will use up more energy than others. The following list shows some examples of the energy a person weighing 60 kg (132 lb) would expend doing the following activities for 30 minutes:

activity	energy
Ironing	69 kcal
Cleaning	75 kcal
Walking	99 kcal
Golf	129 kcal
Fast walking	150 kcal
Cycling	180 kcal
Aerobics	195 kcal
Swimming	195 kcal
Running	300 kcal
Sprinting	405 kcal

effects on the heart and blood that help prevent against cardiovascular disease.

Many of us claim we don't enjoy exercise and simply don't have the time to fit it into our hectic schedules, so the easiest way to increase physical activity is by incorporating it into our daily routines, perhaps by walking or cycling instead of driving (particularly for short journeys), taking up more active hobbies such as gardening, and taking small and simple steps, such as using the stairs instead of the lift whenever possible.

As a general guide, adults should aim to undertake at least 30 minutes of moderate-intensity exercise, such as a brisk walk, five times a week. The 30 minutes does not have to be taken all at once: three sessions

make changes for life

The best way to lose weight is to try to adopt healthier eating habits that you can easily maintain all the time, not just when you are trying to slim down. Aim to lose no more than 1 kg (2 lb) per week to ensure you lose only your fat stores. People who go on crash diets lose lean muscle as well as fat and are much more likely to put the weight back on again soon afterwards.

For a woman, the aim is to reduce her daily calorie intake to around 1,500 kcal while she is trying to lose weight, then settle on around

2,000 per day thereafter to maintain her new body weight. Regular exercise will also make a huge difference.

improve your diet

For most of us, simply adopting a more balanced diet will reduce our calorie intake and lead to weight loss. Follow these simple recommendations:

- Eat more starchy foods, such as bread, potatoes, rice and pasta. Assuming these replace the fattier foods you usually eat, and you don't smother them with oil or butter, this will help reduce the amount of fat and increase the amount of fibre in your diet. As a bonus, try to use wholegrain rice, pasta and flour, as the energy from these foods is released more slowly in the body, making you feel fuller for longer.
- Eat more fruit and vegetables, aiming for at least five portions of different fruit and vegetables a day (excluding potatoes).
- As long as you don't add extra fat to your fruit and vegetables in the form of cream, butter or oil, these changes will help reduce your fat intake and increase the amount of fibre and vitamins you consume.

who said vegetables must be dull?

Eating fewer sugary foods, such as biscuits, cakes and chocolate bars, will help reduce your sugar and fat intake. If you fancy something sweet, aim for fresh or dried fruit instead.

Reduce the amount of fat in your diet, so you consume fewer calories. Choose lean cuts of meat, such as back bacon instead of streaky, and chicken breasts instead of thighs. Trim all visible fat off meat before cooking and avoid frying foods – grill or roast instead. Fish is also naturally low in fat and can make a variety of tempting dishes.

Low-fat versions are available for most dairy products, including milk, cheese, crème fraîche, yogurt, and even cream and butter but low-fat products are normally laden with sugar

13

to make them taste better so it's important to check labels carefully.

simple steps to reduce your calorie intake

Few of us have an iron will, so when you are trying to cut down make it easier on yourself by following these steps:

- Serve small portions to start with. You may feel satisfied when you have finished, but if you are still hungry you can always go back for more.
- Once you have served up your meal, put away any leftover food before you eat. Don't put heaped serving dishes on the table as you will undoubtedly pick, even if you feel satisfied with what you have already eaten.
- Eat slowly and savour your food; then you are more likely to feel full when you have finished. If you rush a meal, you may still feel hungry afterwards.
- Make an effort with your meals. Just because you are cutting down doesn't mean your meals have to be low on taste as well as calories. You will feel more satisfied with a meal you have really enjoyed and will be less likely to look for comfort in a bag of crisps or a bar of chocolate.
- Plan your meals in advance to make sure you have all the ingredients you need. Searching the cupboards when you are hungry is unlikely to result in a healthy, balanced meal.

- Keep healthy and interesting snacks to hand for those moments when you need something to pep you up. You don't need to succumb to a chocolate bar if there are other tempting treats on offer.

sugar

Experts believe it is possible for us as humans to become addicted to sugar, and with an increase in the rates of obesity, diabetes and heart disease in the UK, it's time to look at how we can reduce our intake of a food that we really don't need in our daily diets. Sugar contains no nutrients other than calories, so it provides no protein, vitamins, minerals or essential fats, just pure energy – which is great if you are intending to burn it off, but a lot of us don't, and then it becomes a problem.

how our bodies use sugar

Our bodies digest the sugars we eat using enzymes and acids, finally breaking it down to another type of sugar, called glucose. The stomach and intestines absorb the glucose and then release it into the bloodstream and once there it can be used immediately for energy or stored in the liver and muscle as glycogen for later use.

Insulin (which is made in the pancreas) helps to control the amount of glucose in the bloodstream – it tells the cells to let glucose in when there is too much of it in the bloodstream. As glucose moves from the bloodstream into the cells, blood sugar levels start to drop. The rise and fall of insulin and blood sugar is going on throughout the day and night, and it depends on how much, what and when we eat.

Using glucose for energy and keeping it balanced with just the right amount of insulin is important for helping our bodies function perfectly. The body maintains a minimum level of glucose in the blood, about 70 mg/dl, and also regulates surges of glucose when you eat a meal, to not exceed 140 mg/dl. To conserve fuel, the body stores excess glucose in the liver and muscles, as glycogen. This can then be used when there is no glucose available.

simple and complex sugars

Simple sugars such as pure sugar, honey and syrups metabolize quickly and cause rapid spikes in blood sugar levels, whereas complex sugars such as those found in starchy

vegetables, grains and cereals take longer to digest and therefore give a steadier blood sugar level throughout the day, along with sustained energy. Complex sugars also tend to provide more vitamins and minerals than simple sugars.

how much sugar should we consume?

It is presently recommended that only 10 per cent of our diet should be from added sugar – any more than the amount our body can store as glycogen will turn to fat. This percentage doesn't include sugar that occurs naturally in foods like complex carbohydrates. Fruit, for example, contains fructose (fruit sugar), but whole fruit also contains fibre, which offsets the fructose and makes it healthier for our bodies.

Present surveys show that across all age groups people are consuming 11.5–15.6 per cent of their diets from added sugar, with soft drinks, sweets, jams and alcohol being the biggest culprits.

Scientists are still investigating whether there are direct causal links between high sugar intake and weight gain, type 2 diabetes, heart disease and other illnesses. What is known is that eating too many calories without burning them off through exercise can lead to obesity, and obesity is a risk factor for other diseases.

how to reduce the sugar in your diet

It's important to realize that sugar is in many foods you may not suspect it to be – shop-bought soups, sauces, baked beans, cereals, flavoured yogurts, and even your Chinese takeaway – all contain unnecessary sugar that will add towards your daily total.

Cooking fresh ingredients from scratch enables you to be in control of any added

sugars, and once you start reducing them you will find it becomes easier to go without. Most sugary snacks are eaten out of habit, because they are easily available, so instead be organized and prepared with foods that do not contain sugar. Here are a few tips:

- Cut out added sugar; use only honey and maple syrup in small amounts.
- Don't eat ready-meals or shop-bought sauces or soups – they normally contain sugar, even though you may not taste it.
- Avoid low-fat foods as these products are normally laden with sugar to make them taste better.
- Use herbs and spices for giving extra flavour to your food.
- Choose fresh fruit snacks with small handfuls of nuts or seeds – eating protein with every meal and snack is not only more satiating, it also prevents spikes in blood sugar levels.
- Be aware that so-called healthy breakfast cereals sometimes contain as much as 3 g (⅛ oz) of sugar per 100 g (3½ oz).

16

Make your own breakfast cereal by mixing rolled oats, nuts and seeds together and soaking the mixture in milk in the refrigerator overnight.

- Cinnamon has been shown to help sugar cravings, so use this lovely spice to flavour your cooking and reduce the sugar.
- Drink alcohol in moderation.
- Make a batch of healthy snacks such as Fruit & Nut Slices (see page 38), so you have something to take to work each day rather than be tempted by shop-bought cakes or sweets.
- Drink herbal teas and water with slices of lemon or ginger rather than fizzy drinks or tea/coffee with sugar.

weight loss

Cutting down on your sugar intake should assist with weight loss, but it's still important to eat a healthy, balanced diet, one that includes great protein from meat, fish, eggs, pulses, nuts and seeds, and fresh fruit and vegetables. This book gives a variety of recipes for meals and snacks – and variety

in your diet is very important, to ensure you are consuming a wide range of nutrients that are all-important for optimum health.

Shop-bought foods may contain more sugar to give them extra taste and texture, so again, cooking from scratch enables you to be in control of what you eat and makes it easier to be aware of how much sugar and calories you consume. Portion control is also important, and in this book a calorie intake is given for each recipe to help you to make great-tasting dishes from under 200 to under 500 calories per serving. If you include snacks in your daily intake, just be sure they are healthy choices!

When you are trying to lose weight, the key is to make conscious choices about eating whole, nutritious foods, with a diet that suits your lifestyle, and including exercise to balance what you eat.

recipes under 200 calories

pea, feta & spinach salad

Calories per serving **199**
Serves **4**
Preparation time **10 minutes,
  plus cooling**
Cooking time **2–3 minutes**

2 tablespoons **pumpkin
  seeds**
125 g (4 oz) **fresh** or **frozen
  peas**
30 g (1 oz) **watercress**
3 tablespoons **no added
  sugar mayonnaise**
1 teaspoon **no added sugar
  creamed horseradish**
175 g (6 oz) **feta cheese,
  cubed**
50 g (2 oz) **baby spinach
  leaves**
small handful of **mint leaves**
salt and **pepper**

Heat a nonstick frying pan over a medium-low heat and dry-fry the pumpkin seeds for 2–3 minutes, stirring frequently, until slightly golden and toasted. Leave to cool.

Meanwhile, cook the peas in a saucepan of boiling water until tender. Drain and leave to cool.

Place the watercress, mayonnaise and creamed horseradish in a food processor or blender and blitz until well combined. Season to taste, transfer to a bowl and set aside.

Mix together the feta, peas, spinach, mint leaves and pumpkin seeds in a bowl, then divide on to 4 plates and serve with the watercress mayonnaise.

For pea, mint & feta soup, heat 1 tablespoon olive oil in a saucepan, add 1 chopped onion and cook for 4–5 minutes until softened, then add 250 g (8 oz) frozen peas, 1 peeled and diced potato and 500 ml (17 fl oz) vegetable stock and bring to the boil. Reduce the heat and simmer for 4–5 minutes until the potato is tender. Add a small handful of mint leaves, then using a hand-held blender, blend until smooth. Ladle into 4 bowls and serve sprinkled with 75 g (3 oz) crumbled feta. **Calories per serving 163**

chilli-seared squid & herb salad

Calories per serving **174**
Serves **4**
Preparation time **15 minutes,**
   plus marinating
Cooking time **10 minutes**

large pinch of **sea salt**
1 teaspoon **ground coriander**
1 teaspoon **ground cumin**
1 teaspoon **hot chilli powder**
8 tablespoons **lemon juice**
1 teaspoon **tomato purée**
1 **red chilli**, deseeded and
   finely sliced
1 teaspoon peeled and finely
   grated **fresh root ginger**
1 **garlic clove**, crushed
750 g (1½ lb) **squid**, cut into
   bite-sized pieces
1 small **red onion**, very thinly
   sliced
large handful of **coriander
leaves**, chopped
small handful of **mint leaves,**
   chopped

Mix the salt, ground spices, chilli powder, lemon juice, tomato purée, chilli, ginger and garlic in a large bowl and add the squid. Toss to coat evenly, cover and leave to stand at room temperature for 15 minutes.

Heat a nonstick ridged griddle pan over a very high heat. Working in batches, lift the squid from the marinade and sear in the hot pan for 1–2 minutes, then remove from the pan and keep warm while you cook the remaining squid.

Add the red onion and herbs to the cooked squid, toss to mix well and serve immediately.

For king prawn, mango & herb salad, replace the squid with 750 g (1½ lb) raw peeled king prawns. Marinate in the spice mixture for 10 minutes, then cook in the smoking hot pan in batches for 2–3 minutes on each side, or until pink and cooked through. Transfer to a wide salad bowl and stir in a large handful each of coriander and mint leaves and the diced flesh of 1 mango. Toss to mix well and serve. **Calories per serving 185**

lemon grass, prawn & mint soup

Calories per serving **169**
Serves **4**
Preparation time **15 minutes**
Cooking time **10 minutes**

600 g (1¼ lb) large **raw prawns**, shells on
1.5 litres (2½ pints) **water**
3 tablespoons **soy sauce**
3 **lemon grass stalks**, bruised
2.5 cm (1 inch) piece of **fresh root ginger**, peeled and sliced
1 **red chilli**, deseeded and sliced
4 **kaffir lime leaves**, shredded
100 g (3½ oz) **rice noodles**
2 tablespoons shredded **mint**
lime wedges, to serve (optional)

Peel the prawns and set aside. Place the shells, heads and tails in a saucepan and heat until the shells are well coloured. Add the measurement water and bring to the boil, then reduce the heat and simmer for 2 minutes. Strain through a sieve and return the stock to the pan, discarding the contents of the sieve.

Add the soy sauce, lemon grass, ginger, chilli and lime leaves to the stock and simmer for 5 minutes.

Meanwhile, cook the rice noodles according to the packet instructions.

Add the prawns to the broth and cook for 2–3 minutes until they turn pink and are cooked through.

Divide the rice noodles between 4 bowls. Stir the mint into the soup, then pour over the noodles. Serve with lime wedges for squeezing over, if liked.

For asparagus, lemon grass & prawn stir-fry, mix together 1 tablespoon peeled and grated fresh root ginger, 1 bruised and finely chopped lemon grass stalk, 4 sliced lime leaves and 3 tablespoons no added sugar fish sauce. Heat a wok and add 1 tablespoon groundnut oil. Cook 10 raw peeled king prawns for 2–3 minutes until they turn pink, then remove from the pan. Add 1 sliced onion, 2 sliced red chillies, 3 chopped spring onions and 3 chopped garlic cloves to the pan and stir-fry for 4 minutes. Return the prawns to the pan with 250 g (8 oz) trimmed and halved asparagus stalks and fry for 1 minute. Pour in the spiced sauce and cook for a further 1 minute, then serve. **Calories per serving 107**

avocado & soured cream soup

Calories per serving **170**
Serves **6**
Preparation time **15 minutes**
Cooking time **5 minutes**

1 tablespoon **sunflower oil**
4 **spring onions**, sliced, plus
    2 extra to garnish
2 large ripe **avocados**, halved
    and stoned
4 tablespoons **soured cream**
600 ml (1 pint) **vegetable** or
    chicken stock
juice of 2 **limes**
few drops of **Tabasco sauce**
salt and **pepper**
ice cubes, to serve

Heat the oil in a frying pan, add the spring onions and fry for 5 minutes until softened. Set aside.

Cut very thin strips from the 2 extra spring onions to create curls. Soak in cold water for 10 minutes, then drain.

Scoop out the avocado flesh from the shells and add to a blender or food processor with the fried spring onions, the soured cream and about a third of the stock. Blend to a smooth purée, then gradually mix in the remaining stock and lime juice. Season to taste with salt, pepper and a few drops of Tabasco sauce.

Serve the soup immediately, while the avocado is still bright green, in 6 cups or glass tumblers containing some ice. Scatter the spring onion curls over the soup.

For homemade salt & pepper grissini, to serve as an accompaniment, put 250 g (8 oz) strong white flour into a bowl and mix with ¼ teaspoon salt, 1 teaspoon maple syrup and 1 teaspoon fast-action dried yeast. Add 4 teaspoons olive oil and gradually mix in up to 150 ml (¼ pint) warm water to form a smooth dough. Knead for 5 minutes on a lightly floured surface, then cut the dough into 18 pieces and roll each into a thin rope. Place on a greased baking sheet, cover with oiled clingfilm and leave in a warm place to rise for 30 minutes. Remove the clingfilm, brush the bread with beaten egg, then sprinkle with a little coarse sea salt and a generous scattering of roughly crushed black peppercorns. Bake in a preheated oven, 200°C (400°F), Gas Mark 6, for 6–8 minutes until golden. Serve warm or cold with the soup. **Calories per grissini 57**

scallops with minty pea purée

Calories per serving **152**
Serves **4**
Preparation time **5 minutes**
Cooking time **10 minutes**

2 tablespoons **olive oil**
4 **shallots**, finely diced
300 g (10 oz) **frozen peas**
100 ml (3½ fl oz) **fish stock**
small handful of **mint leaves**
1 tablespoon **crème fraîche**
grated rind and juice of 1
   lemon
12 cleaned **scallops**
salt and **pepper**

Heat 1 tablespoon of the oil in a small pan, add the shallots and fry for 4–5 minutes until softened. Stir in the peas and stock and cook until the peas have heated through. Transfer to a food processor or blender, add the mint leaves, crème fraîche, lemon rind and salt and pepper and blend until smooth.

Meanwhile, heat the remaining oil in a frying pan or griddle pan, add the scallops and cook for 2 minutes on each side until cooked through, squeezing with lemon juice after turning them over.

Divide the pea purée between 4 plates, top with the scallops and a drizzle of the cooking juices.

For pan-fried scallops with lime & coriander, heat 1 tablespoon olive oil in a frying pan, add 12 cleaned scallops and cook for 2 minutes. Flip the scallops over, then sprinkle with 2 large chopped garlic cloves and 1 deseeded and chopped red chilli and cook for 1 minute until just cooked through. Squeeze over the juice of 1 lime, then stir in a handful of chopped coriander and season with salt and pepper. Serve immediately. **Calories per serving 69**

poached chicken & vegetables

Calories per serving **195**
Serves **4**
Preparation time **10 minutes**
Cooking time **25 minutes**

2 **fennel bulbs**, thinly sliced
4 **boneless, skinless chicken breasts**, about 150 g (5 oz)
each, sliced diagonally into
3 pieces
grated rind and juice of 1
lemon
600 ml (1 pint) **chicken stock**
1 **courgette**, sliced
2 tablespoons chopped
parsley

Place the fennel, chicken, lemon rind and juice and stock in a wok or large saucepan and bring to the boil, then reduce the heat and simmer, uncovered, for 15 minutes.

Add the courgette and half the parsley and cook for a further 5 minutes until the courgette is tender and the chicken is cooked through.

Serve sprinkled with the remaining parsley.

For lemon, courgette & chicken pasta, cook 350 g (11½ oz) gluten-free wholemeal pasta in a saucepan of boiling water according to the packet instructions. Meanwhile, heat 15 g (½ oz) butter in a frying pan, add 3 coarsely grated courgettes and fry for 5 minutes until softened. Add 200 g (7 oz) shredded ready-cooked chicken and cook for 2–3 minutes until heated through. Drain the pasta, then stir into the chicken mixture with 2 tablespoons olive oil, 4 thinly sliced spring onions, the juice and grated rind of 1 lemon and pepper. **Calories per serving 476**

ranch-style eggs

Calories per serving **188**
Serves **4**
Preparation time **10 minutes**
Cooking time **15 minutes**

2 tablespoons **olive oil**
1 **onion**, finely sliced
1 **red chilli,** deseeded and
    finely chopped
1 **garlic clove**, crushed
1 teaspoon **ground cumin**
1 teaspoon **dried oregano**
400 g (13 oz) can **cherry
    tomatoes**
200 g (7 oz) **roasted red** and
    yellow peppers in oil (from
    a jar), drained and roughly
    chopped
4 **eggs**
salt and **pepper**
4 tablespoons finely chopped
    coriander, to garnish

Heat the oil in a large frying pan, add the onion, chilli, garlic, cumin and oregano and fry gently for about 5 minutes until softened.

Add the tomatoes and peppers and cook for a further 5 minutes. If the sauce looks dry, add a splash of water.

Season well and make 4 hollows in the mixture, then break an egg into each and cover the pan. Cook for 5 minutes, or until the eggs are just set.

Serve immediately, garnished with the chopped coriander and sprinkled with extra pepper.

For Mexican-style scrambled eggs, heat 1 tablespoon each olive oil and butter in a large frying pan. Whisk together 8 eggs, 1 crushed garlic clove, 1 finely chopped red chilli, 1 teaspoon dried oregano and 1 teaspoon ground cumin in a bowl. Season, pour into the frying pan and cook over a medium-low heat, stirring frequently, until the eggs are scrambled and cooked to your liking. Serve sprinkled with chopped coriander. **Calories per serving 230**

aubergine curry

Calories per serving **108**
Serves **4**
Preparation time **10 minutes**
Cooking time **35–40 minutes**

800 g (1¾ lb) **aubergines**
1 tablespoon **olive oil**
1 **onion**, sliced
1 **green chilli**, deseeded and
   sliced
2 **garlic cloves**, crushed
2.5 cm (1 inch) piece of **fresh
   root ginger**, peeled and
   shredded
400 g (13 oz) can **chopped
   tomatoes**
1 tablespoon **tomato purée**
1 teaspoon **ground cumin**
1 teaspoon **ground coriander**
small bunch of **coriander**,
   chopped
salt and **pepper**
4 tablespoons **low-fat natural
   yogurt**, to serve

Prick the aubergines all over with a fork and bake in a preheated oven, 220°C (425°F), Gas Mark 7, for 20 minutes until the skin is blackened. When cool enough to handle, peel off the skin and roughly chop the flesh.

Heat the oil in a frying pan, add the onion and fry for 3–4 minutes until starting to soften. Stir in the chilli, garlic and ginger and cook for a further 2–3 minutes.

Add the aubergine, chopped tomatoes, tomato purée and dried spices and cook for a further 10–12 minutes. Season to taste, then stir in the chopped coriander.

Serve with dollops of natural yogurt.

For baba ganoush, prick 2 large aubergines all over with a fork. Grill or bake as above for 15–20 minutes until the skins are blackened and the flesh feels soft. Place 2 peeled garlic cloves, the juice of 1 lemon, 2 tablespoons tahini, 2 tablespoons olive oil and salt and pepper in a food processor or blender and blend together. When cool enough to handle, cut the aubergines in half and scoop out the flesh. Mix with the smooth paste and serve with a sprinkling of chopped parsley. **Calories per serving 137**

vegetable stroganoff

Calories per serving **159**
Serves **4**
Preparation time **15 minutes**
Cooking time **20 minutes**

1 tablespoon **olive oil**
1 **onion**, diced
2 **garlic cloves**, finely chopped
175 g (6 oz) **butternut squash,** peeled, deseeded and diced
1 **carrot**, peeled and diced
100 g (3½ oz) **celeriac**, peeled and diced
100 g (3½ oz) **shiitake mushrooms**, sliced
½ teaspoon **paprika**
200 ml (7 fl oz) **vegetable stock**
400 g (13 oz) can **kidney beans**, rinsed and drained
2 tablespoons **natural yogurt**
2 tablespoons chopped **parsley**
salt and **pepper**

Heat the oil in a saucepan, add the onion and garlic and fry for 2 minutes until starting to soften. Add the butternut, carrot, celeriac, mushrooms and paprika and cook for a further 2–3 minutes.

Pour in the stock, cover and simmer for 10 minutes, then add the beans and cook for a further 5 minutes until all the vegetables are tender.

Stir in the yogurt and parsley and season to taste.

For roasted vegetable salad, toss together the onion, garlic, butternut squash and celeriac in a large bowl, then add 2 peeled and diced carrots and 1 thickly sliced courgette. Toss together with 2 tablespoons olive oil and 1 teaspoon smoked paprika. Divide between 2 roasting tins and roast in a preheated oven, 200°C (400°F), Gas Mark 6, for 30–35 minutes until tender. Toss the roasted vegetables with 100 g (3½ oz) baby spinach leaves and serve with a squeeze of lemon juice and grinding of pepper. **Calories per serving 80**

fruit & nut slices

Calories per slice **99**
Makes **16**
Preparation time **10 minutes**
Cooking time **20 minutes**

butter, for greasing
1 large **carrot**, peeled and
  chopped
1 **dessert apple**, quartered
  and cored
½ teaspoon **ground
  cinnamon**
½ teaspoon **ground nutmeg**
225 g (7½ oz) **cooked brown
  rice**
2 **eggs**
90 ml (3 fl oz) **water**
115 g (4 oz) **rice flour**
55 g (2 oz) **raisins**
55 g (2 oz) **hazelnuts**,
  chopped
1 tablespoon **sesame seeds**

Grease a 30 x 20 cm (12 x 8 inch) baking tin and line
with nonstick baking paper.

Place the carrot, apple, spices, rice, eggs and
measurement water in a food processor or blender and
blend until quite smooth. Add the rice flour and blend
again, then add the raisins and nuts and process for
10 seconds until just chopped.

Transfer the mixture to the prepared tin, sprinkle with
the sesame seeds and mark into 16 slices. Bake in
a preheated oven, 200°C (400°F), Gas Mark 6, for
20 minutes until lightly golden. Leave to cool in the
tin, then remove the lining paper and break into slices.
Store in an airtight container and eat within 3–4 days.

For fruit & nut bircher muesli, mix together 200 g
(7 oz) rolled oats, 2 tablespoons raisins, 2 tablespoons
chopped pitted dates, 1 tablespoon pumpkin seeds,
1 tablespoon toasted walnut halves, 1 teaspoon
ground cinnamon, 1 tablespoon chopped hazelnuts
and 1 tablespoon desiccated coconut in a bowl. Grate
1 dessert apple into the mixture and stir in 300 ml
(½ pint) semi-skimmed milk and leave to soak in
the refrigerator overnight. Divide the muesli between
4 bowls, top each with a handful of fresh berries and
serve with extra milk, if liked. **Calories per serving 173
(not including extra milk)**

poppy seed & lemon cupcakes

Calories per cake **170**
Makes **12**
Preparation time **20 minutes,
  plus cooling**
Cooking time about **1 hour**

2 **unwaxed lemons**
100 g (3½ oz) **ground
  hazelnuts**
50 g (2 oz) **spelt flour**
1 teaspoon **baking powder**
2 tablespoons **poppy seeds**
3 **eggs**
5 tablespoons **agave nectar**,
  plus extra for drizzling
50 g (2 oz) **lightly salted
  butter**, melted
50 g (2 oz) **sultanas**

Line a 12-hole bun tray with paper cake cases. Cut one lemon into 12 thin slices. Put with the whole lemon in a small saucepan and cover with boiling water. Simmer very gently for 20–30 minutes until the slices are tender. Drain the slices and reserve. Cook the whole lemon for a further 15 minutes until soft and squashy. Drain and leave to cool.

Halve the whole lemon and discard the pips. Roughly chop, put in a food processor or blender and blend to a purée.

Mix the ground hazelnuts in a bowl with the flour, baking powder and poppy seeds. Mix the eggs with the lemon purée, agave nectar and melted butter and add to the dry ingredients with the sultanas. Stir until evenly combined.

Divide the cake mixture between the paper cases and place a reserved lemon slice on top. Drizzle each lemon slice with a little extra agave nectar.

Bake in a preheated oven, 180°C (350°F), Gas Mark 4, for 20 minutes, or until risen and lightly browned. Transfer to a wire rack to cool.

For Brazil nut & orange cupcakes, cook 1 small orange as above. Drain, put in a food processor or blender with the eggs, melted butter, agave nectar and sultanas and blend to a purée. Chop and then grind 100 g (3½ oz) Brazil nuts. Mix with the flour and baking powder as above, adding ½ teaspoon ground allspice (omit the poppy seeds). Combine with the orange purée mixture and bake as above, with a whole Brazil nut on top of each cake. **Calories per cake 180**

banana & raspberry ice cream

Calories per serving **92**
(including maple syrup)
Serves **4**
Preparation time **10 minutes,
plus freezing**

2 **bananas**, cut into 5 mm
(¼ inch) slices
100 g (3½ oz) **raspberries**
2 tablespoons **coconut cream**
1 tablespoon **maple syrup**
(optional)

Put the banana slices in a single layer on a tray, then place in the freezer with the raspberries and freeze for at least 2 hours.

Put a few of the frozen banana pieces in a food processor and blitz, then with the motor still running, through the feeder tube gradually add more banana pieces, a few raspberries, a drizzle of coconut cream and maple syrup, if using. Continue to add the ingredients until they are all used and the ice cream is thick and creamy.

Serve immediately or transfer to a freezerproof container and place in the freezer for up to 1 hour before serving. (If left in the freezer too long, the ice cream will set quite hard and will need to be left to stand for about 20 minutes before serving.)

For banana & mango ice cream, slice 3 bananas and freeze in a single layer as above. Peel, stone and dice 1 large mango, then freeze as above. Pour 140 ml (4½ fl oz) almond milk into a food processor and switch to full power. Gradually add the banana and mango pieces as above and blend until the ice cream is smooth and creamy. **Calories per serving 119**

berry & mint compote

Calories per serving **97**
Serves **4**
Preparation time **5 minutes,
  plus cooling**
Cooking time **12–15 minutes**

450 g (14½ oz) **mixed
  fruit**, such as strawberries,
  blackberries, raspberries and
  halved and stoned plums
1 **cinnamon stick**
grated rind and juice of 1
  orange
8 **mint leaves**, shredded
320 g (11 oz) **natural yogurt,**
  to serve (optional)

Place the fruit, cinnamon stick and orange rind and juice in a small saucepan and simmer gently for 12–15 minutes.

Remove the cinnamon stick and leave the compote to cool for 3–4 minutes, then stir in the mint. Spoon into 4 bowls, divide the natural yogurt between them, if liked, and serve.

For berry & mint smoothies, place 400 g (13 oz) natural yogurt, 400 ml (14 fl oz) soya milk, 5–6 ice cubes, 300 g (10 oz) mixed raspberries, blueberries and hulled strawberries and 5–6 mint leaves in a food processor or blender and blend until smooth. Pour into 4 glasses and serve topped with mint sprigs. **Calories per serving 119**

melon with mint & ginger syrup

Calories per serving **108**
Serves **4**
Preparation time **5 minutes,**
   plus standing
Cooking time **5 minutes**

1 tablespoon **sesame seeds**
½ **honeydew melon**, peeled,
   deseeded and cut into large
   chunks
½ **cantaloupe melon**, peeled,
   deseeded and cut into large
   chunks
3 tablespoons **maple syrup**
1 tablespoon **water**
2 tablespoons **shredded mint**
1 tablespoon peeled and
   shredded **fresh root ginger**

Heat a nonstick frying pan over a medium-low heat and dry-fry the sesame seeds for 2 minutes, stirring frequently, until golden brown and toasted. Set aside.

Place the melon chunks on a large serving plate.

Pour the maple syrup into a pan with the measurement water and bring to the boil, then add the mint and ginger and turn off the heat. Leave to stand for 5 minutes, then pour over the melon.

Sprinkle with the toasted sesame seeds and serve.

For melon & ginger smoothies, place the flesh of 1 cantaloupe melon in a blender with ½ teaspoon ground ginger, a pinch of nutmeg, 2 tablespoons Greek yogurt and 900 ml (1½ pints) semi-skimmed milk. Blend until smooth, then pour into 4 glasses and serve. **Calories per serving 157**

banana rice pudding

Calories per serving **162**
Serves **4**
Preparation time **5 minutes**
Cooking time about **2 hours**

butter, for greasing
50 g (2 oz) **dried banana**,
   broken into small pieces
50 g (2 oz) **pudding rice**
750 ml (1¼ pints) **milk**
large pinch of freshly grated
   nutmeg

Grease a 900 ml (1½ pint) ovenproof dish lightly with butter and place the banana pieces and pudding rice in the dish.

Heat the milk in a small saucepan until it reaches boiling point, then pour over the bananas and rice and stir to mix. Sprinkle with the grated nutmeg.

Bake in a preheated oven, 150°C (300°F), Gas Mark 2, for 1¾–2 hours until the rice is tender and most of the milk has been absorbed, stirring once halfway through cooking.

For quick banana mousse, mash 4 ripe bananas with 2 tablespoons maple syrup or honey in a bowl. Stir in 500 g (1 lb) Greek yogurt, then spoon evenly into 4 bowls or glasses and top with 1 tablespoon broken dried banana pieces. **Calories per serving 251**

mixed fruit salad

Calories per serving **125**
Serves **6**
Preparation time **15 minutes**

¼ **watermelon**, peeled and
   deseeded
½ **galia melon**, peeled and
   deseeded
1 **mango**, peeled and stoned
2 **green dessert apples**,
   quartered and cored
2 **bananas**
3 **kiwifruit**, peeled
200 g (7 oz) **strawberries**,
   hulled
150 g (5 oz) **blueberries**

Cut the melon flesh into 2–3 cm (1 inch) chunks and
place in a large bowl.

Dice the mango and apples, then slice the bananas.
Add to the bowl with the melon.

Cut the kiwifruit flesh into rounds, then add to the bowl
with the berries and mix the fruit together carefully.

For passion fruit cream, to serve as an accompaniment,
whisk together 4 tablespoons mascarpone cheese and
200 ml (7 fl oz) double cream in a bowl until soft peaks
form. Gently fold in the pulp of 2 passion fruit. **Calories
per serving 197**

lemon & blueberry pancakes

Calories per pancake **107**
Makes **12**
Preparation time **10 minutes**
Cooking time **10–20 minutes**

250 g (8 oz) **self-raising wholemeal flour**
grated rind of 1 **lemon**
2 **eggs**, beaten
300 ml (½ pint) **semi-skimmed milk**
300 g (10 oz) **blueberries**

To serve
lemon juice
2 tablespoons **maple syrup**

Place the flour and lemon rind in a bowl and make a well in the centre. Pour the eggs into the well, then whisk together, gradually adding the milk to form a smooth batter. Stir in half the blueberries.

Heat a nonstick pan over a medium heat, add 3–4 tablespoons of the batter to form individual pancakes and cook for 1–2 minutes until golden underneath, then flip over and cook for a further 1–2 minutes. Remove from the pan and keep warm. Repeat with the remaining batter to make 12 pancakes.

Serve sprinkled with the remaining blueberries, a squeeze of lemon juice and drizzle of maple syrup.

For lemon & blueberry pots, lightly crush 300 g (10 oz) blueberries in a bowl until some of them burst. Stir in 500 g (1 lb) Greek yogurt and the grated rind of 1 lemon. Divide between 4 small glasses or bowls and sprinkle with 1 tablespoon toasted flaked almonds to serve. **Calories per serving 194**

chargrilled fruit with chilli salt

Calories per serving **72**
Serves **6**
Preparation time **15 minutes**
Cooking time **6 minutes**

1 large **mango**, peeled and
stoned
½ **pineapple**, skin removed
and cored
2 **bananas**
½ teaspoon **dried chilli flakes**
1 tablespoon **sea salt** or
vanilla sea salt

Cut the mango into 2 cm (¾ inch) pieces and the pineapple into small wedges. Cut the bananas into thick slices.

Thread the fruit on to 6 metal or presoaked wooden skewers, alternating the fruits.

Mix together the chilli and salt and set aside.

Heat a griddle pan over a medium heat, add the skewers and cook for 3 minutes on each side until golden and caramelized. Remove the skewers from the pan, sprinkle with the chilli salt mix and serve.

For vanilla sea salt, to accompany the skewers, scrape the seeds of 1 vanilla pod into a small bowl with 4 tablespoons sea salt. Stir to combine well and leave to infuse for at least 2 hours. **Calories per serving negligible**

papaya with tumbling berries

Calories per serving **92 (not including honey)**
Serves **4**
Preparation time **8 minutes**

2 large **papayas**
125 g (4 oz) **blueberries**
125 g (4 oz) **raspberries**
250 g (8 oz) **strawberries**, sliced
125 g (4 oz) **cherries**, pitted
clear honey, to taste (optional)
lime wedges, to serve

Cut the papayas in half, then scoop out the seeds and discard. Place each half on a serving plate.

Mix together the blueberries, raspberries, strawberries and cherries in a bowl and then pile into the papaya halves. Drizzle with a little honey, if liked, and serve with lime wedges.

For papaya & berry smoothies, peel and halve the papayas, remove the seeds and cut into chunks. Place in a food processor or blender with the remaining fruits and 10 ice cubes. Add 500 ml (17 fl oz) pure apple or guava juice and blend until smooth. Pour into 4 glasses and serve immediately. **Calories per serving 144**

pineapple & grapefruit with mint

Calories per serving **161**
Serves **4**
Preparation time **10 minutes,
  plus cooling**
Cooking time **5 minutes**

2 tablespoons **honey**
juice of ½ **lime**
1 tablespoon **water**
2 **pink grapefruit**
1 small **pineapple**
small bunch of **mint**, leaves
  only, shredded
4 tablespoons **natural yogurt**,
  to serve

Place the honey, lime juice and measurement water in a small saucepan and slowly bring to a simmer, then stir, turn off the heat and leave to cool.

Segment the grapefruit over a bowl to catch the juices. Remove the skin from the pineapple, cut into quarters and remove the core. Cut into thin slices, adding any juice to the grapefruit juices. Arrange the fruit on a serving platter.

Stir the reserved fruit juices and the mint into the honey mixture, then pour over the fruit. Serve with the natural yogurt.

For glazed spiced pineapple, mix together the juice and grated rind of 1 lime, 2 tablespoons clear honey and a couple of pinches of ground cinnamon in a bowl. Peel and core 1 pineapple as above, then cut into 8 wedges. Heat 20 g (¾ oz) butter in a frying pan and cook the pineapple wedges for 3–4 minutes, turning frequently, until caramelized. Pour in the spiced lime sauce and let it bubble for a few seconds, turning the pineapple in the sauce. Divide between 4 plates and serve each with 1 tablespoon crème fraîche. **Calories per serving 385**

chillied melon foam

Calories per serving **72**
Serves **6**
Preparation time **15 minutes**

2 **Galia melons**
juice of 1 **lime**
½–1 large mild **red chilli**,
    deseeded and quartered
small bunch of **coriander**, plus
    extra sprigs to decorate
300 ml (½ pint) **pressed**
    apple juice
ice cubes, to serve
lime wedges, to decorate
    (optional)

Cut the melons in half, scoop out and discard the seeds, then scoop the flesh away from the skin and put it into a blender or food processor with the lime juice, chilli and coriander, torn into pieces. Add half the apple juice and blend until smooth. Gradually mix in the remaining juice until frothy.

Pour the melon foam into 6 cups or glass tumblers half filled with ice and serve immediately, decorated with a sprig of coriander and lime wedges, if liked, before the foamy texture loses its bubbles.

balsamic & pepper strawberries

Calories per serving **41**
Serves **4**
Preparation time **5 minutes**

500g (1 lb) **strawberries**,
   hulled and halved
2 tablespoons **balsamic
   vinegar**
1 teaspoon freshly ground
   pepper

Place the strawberries in a bowl and pour over
the vinegar.

Stir well, to incorporate the flavours, then add the
pepper to taste. Serve immediately.

apple & pear tart

Calories per serving **152**
Serves **8**
Preparation time **15 minutes**
Cooking time **10–15 minutes**

130 g (4½ oz) **rice flour**
150 g (5 oz) **ground almonds**
1 tablespoon **tahini**
½ tablespoon **sunflower oil**
100 ml (3½ fl oz) **cold water**
4 **dessert apples**, peeled,
  cored and chopped
50 g (2 oz) **pitted dates**
1½ teaspoons **ground
  cinnamon**
2 **pears**, peeled, cored and
  thinly sliced
juice of 1 **lemon**

Place the rice flour, ground almonds, tahini and oil in a food processor and process until the mixture resembles breadcrumbs. With the motor still running, slowly add the measurement water though the feeder tube until the mixture comes together like pastry.

Line a 20 cm (8 inch) tart tin with the pastry, using your fingers to push it to the edges. Bake in a preheated oven, 180°C (350°F), Gas Mark 4, for 10–15 minutes until golden.

Meanwhile, place the apples, dates and 1 teaspoon of the cinnamon in a small saucepan with 2 tablespoons water and cook over a gentle heat until the apples are soft. Transfer to a food processor or blender and blend to a purée, then spread over the base of the pastry case.

Toss the pears in the lemon juice, then arrange them in a spiral over the apple mixture. Sprinkle with the remaining cinnamon to serve.

For apple & pear fool, peel, core and chop 3 dessert apples and 2 pears. Place in a saucepan with 6 pitted dates, 1 teaspoon ground cinnamon, the grated rind and juice of 1 orange and 150 ml (¼ pint) water. Cook over a gentle heat until the apples and pears are soft. Blend as above until smooth and leave to cool. Fold into 500 g (1 lb) low-fat natural yogurt and spoon into 4 glasses or bowls. Chill for 20 minutes before serving. **Calories per serving 213**

recipes
under 300
calories

crab & grapefruit salad

Calories per serving **253**
Serves **4**
Preparation time **15 minutes**
Cooking time **2 minutes**

2 tablespoons **sesame seeds**
2 **pink grapefruit**
3 tablespoons **extra virgin olive oil**
1 teaspoon **clear honey**
1 teaspoon **Dijon mustard**
350 g (11½ oz) **white crabmeat**
60 g (2¼ oz) **watercress**
100 g (3½ oz) **mangetout**
small handful of **coriander leaves**
salt and **pepper**

Heat a nonstick frying pan over a medium-low heat and dry-fry the sesame seeds for 2 minutes, stirring frequently, until golden brown and toasted. Set aside.

Segment the grapefruit over a bowl to catch the juice.

Whisk together 2 tablespoons of the grapefruit juice with the olive oil, honey and mustard in a small bowl. Season with salt and pepper.

Mix 1 tablespoon of the dressing with the crabmeat.

Divide the watercress, mangetout, grapefruit segments and coriander leaves between 4 plates and top with the crabmeat.

Sprinkle with the toasted sesame seeds and the remaining dressing and serve.

For spiced potted crab, mix together 300 g (10 oz) crabmeat, 100 g (3½ oz) melted butter, ½ deseeded and finely chopped red chilli, the juice of 1 lemon, ½ teaspoon grated nutmeg and a pinch of salt in a bowl, then pack into a 400 g (13 oz) jar. Melt 75 g (3 oz) butter until it is foaming. Remove from the heat and skim off the scum with a teaspoon. Pour the clear butter over the crab, top with a bay leaf and leave to set in the refrigerator for 1 hour before serving with gluten-free crispbreads, if liked. **Calories per serving 384 (not including crispbreads)**

squash, kale & mixed bean soup

Calories per serving **243 (not including garlic bread)**
Serves **6**
Preparation time **15 minutes**
Cooking time **40 minutes**

1 tablespoon **olive oil**
1 **onion**, finely chopped
2 **garlic cloves**, finely chopped
1 teaspoon **smoked paprika**
500 g (1 lb) **butternut squash**, peeled, deseeded and diced
2 small **carrots**, peeled and diced
500 g (1 lb) **tomatoes**, skinned, if liked, and roughly chopped
410 g (13½ oz) can **mixed beans**, rinsed and drained
900 ml (1½ pints) **vegetable** or **chicken stock**
150 ml (¼ pint) **crème fraîche**
100 g (3½ oz) **kale**, torn into bite-sized pieces
salt and **pepper**

Heat the oil in a saucepan, add the onion and fry gently for 5 minutes. Stir in the garlic and smoked paprika and cook briefly, then add the squash, carrots, tomatoes and mixed beans.

Pour in the stock, season with salt and pepper and bring to the boil, stirring. Cover and simmer for 25 minutes until the vegetables are tender.

Stir the crème fraîche into the soup, then add the kale, pressing it just beneath the surface of the stock. Cover and cook for 5 minutes until the kale has just wilted. Ladle into 6 bowls and serve with warm garlic bread, if liked.

For cheesy squash, pepper & mixed bean soup, fry the onion in oil as above, add the garlic, smoked paprika, squash, tomatoes and beans, adding a cored, deseeded and diced red pepper instead of the carrot. Pour in the stock, then add 65 g (2½ oz) Parmesan rinds and season. Cover and simmer for 25 minutes. Stir in the crème fraîche but omit the kale. Discard the Parmesan rinds, ladle the soup into 6 bowls and top each with 15 g (½ oz) freshly grated Parmesan. **Calories per serving 301**

potato & avocado salad

Calories per serving **281**
Serves **4**
Preparation time **10 minutes**
Cooking time **12–15 minutes**

600 g (1 ¼ lb) small **new
    potatoes**
1 **avocado**
1 punnet **mustard and cress**
grated rind of ½ **lemon**
75 g (3 oz) **rocket leaves**
salt and **pepper**

Dressing
1 tablespoon **no added sugar
    wholegrain mustard**
juice of ½ **lemon**
2 tablespoons **no added
    sugar mayonnaise**

Cook the potatoes in a saucepan of salted boiling water for 12–15 minutes, or until just tender. Drain well and place in a large salad bowl.

Halve the avocado, remove the stone and peel. Cut the flesh into pieces. Whisk together the dressing ingredients in a small bowl, then add to the warm potatoes. Mix in the avocado pieces, mustard and cress, lemon rind and rocket. Season well.

Divide the salad between 4 bowls or plates and serve.

For potato & sun-dried tomato salad, cook the potatoes as above, drain well and place in a large salad bowl. While they are still warm, stir in 6 sliced, drained sun-dried tomatoes in oil, 12 sliced pitted olives, 2 tablespoons pesto and 3 tablespoons light crème fraîche. Season with plenty of pepper. **Calories per serving 252**

fennel vichyssoise

Calories per serving **209**
Serves **6**
Preparation time **20 minutes,
plus chilling**
Cooking time **30 minutes**

25 g (1 oz) **butter**
1 **fennel bulb**, about
    200–250 g (7–8 oz), green
    feathery tops trimmed and
    reserved, bulb roughly
    chopped
4 **spring onions**, thickly sliced
150 g (5 oz) **potato**, diced
450 ml (¾ pint) **chicken stock**
250 ml (8 fl oz) **milk**
150 ml (¼ pint) **double cream**
salt and **pepper**
ice cubes, to serve

Heat the butter in a saucepan, add the chopped fennel, spring onions and potato, toss in the butter, then cover and fry gently for 10 minutes, stirring occasionally, until softened but not browned.

Pour in the stock, season and bring to the boil. Cover and simmer for 15 minutes until the vegetables are just tender and still tinged green.

Leave the soup to cool slightly, then purée in batches in a blender or food processor until smooth. Pour the purée through a fine sieve back into the saucepan, then press the coarser pieces of fennel through the sieve using the back of a ladle. Mix in the milk and cream, then taste and adjust the seasoning if needed. Chill well.

Ladle the soup into 6 small bowls or cups half filled with ice and garnish with the reserved green feathery tops, snipped into small pieces.

For classic vichyssoise, omit the fennel and spring onions and add 375 g (12 oz) trimmed, cleaned and sliced leeks. Stir half the cream into the soup and swirl the rest through the bowls before serving. Garnish with a sprinkling of a few snipped chives. **Calories per serving 215**

spinach & feta quiches

Calories per serving **274**
Serves **4**
Preparation time **15 minutes**
Cooking time **12–15 minutes**

400 g (13 oz) **spinach**
6 large **eggs**
100 ml (3½ fl oz) **milk**
2 tablespoons grated
   Parmesan cheese
2 tablespoons chopped
   chives
100 g (3½ oz) **feta cheese**,
   cubed or crumbled
8 **cherry tomatoes**, halved
salt and **pepper**
crisp green salad, to serve

Place the spinach in a sieve and pour over boiling water to wilt. Squeeze out any excess liquid. Line 8 holes of a muffin tin with 15 cm (6 inch) squares of greaseproof paper.

Beat together the eggs, milk, Parmesan, chives and feta in a jug and season with salt and pepper.

Divide the spinach between the muffin cases, then pour in the egg mixture. Top each one with 2 tomato halves.

Bake in a preheated oven, 180°C (350°F), Gas Mark 4, for 12–15 minutes until just set. Serve with a crisp green salad.

For spinach & feta frittata, whisk 7 large eggs in a bowl and season with salt and pepper. Heat 1 tablespoon olive oil in a frying pan, add 4 sliced spring onions and cook for 2–3 minutes. Add 150 g (5 oz) spinach and toss in the hot oil to wilt. Add to the beaten eggs and mix well. Crumble in 200 g (7 oz) feta cheese. Heat 1 tablespoon olive oil in the frying pan, pour in the egg mixture and cook over a medium heat until nearly set, then place under a preheated hot grill until cooked and golden on top. Serve cut into 4 wedges. **Calories per serving 345**

spicy falafel with mint raita

Calories per serving **212**
Serves **4**
Preparation time **15 minutes,
plus chilling**
Cooking time **20 minutes**

2 tablespoons **groundnut oil**
1 small **onion**, finely diced
2 **garlic cloves**, crushed
400 g (13 oz) can **chickpeas**,
rinsed and drained
1 teaspoon **ground cumin**
½ teaspoon **ground coriander**
small handful of **coriander**,
chopped
small handful of **parsley**,
chopped
salt and **pepper**

Raita
300 g (10 oz) **natural yogurt**
½ **cucumber**, grated
small handful of **mint**, chopped

Heat 1 tablespoon of the oil in a frying pan, add the onion and garlic and fry for 4–5 minutes until softened.

Transfer the onion and garlic to a food processor or blender, add the chickpeas, spices and salt and pepper, then process to a coarse mixture. Add the herbs and pulse until combined. Chill for 30 minutes.

Meanwhile, make the raita. Mix together the yogurt, cucumber and mint in a bowl. Cover and chill.

Roll the chickpea mixture into about 32 balls, then flatten to make small patties. Heat the remaining oil in a frying pan, add the patties, in batches if necessary, and fry for 3 minutes on each side until golden and firm. Serve with the raita.

For chickpea & mint soup, heat 1 tablespoon olive oil in a frying pan, add 1 chopped onion, 2 chopped celery sticks and 2 chopped garlic cloves and cook for 4–5 minutes until softened. Add a rinsed and drained 400 g (13 oz) can chickpeas, 1 chopped bunch of mint, ½ teaspoon ground cumin, 1 tablespoon tahini and 750 ml (1¼ pints) vegetable stock. Bring to the boil, then reduce the heat and simmer for 30 minutes. Season, then mash lightly with a potato masher. Ladle into 4 bowls and serve each topped with 40 g (1½ oz) low-fat natural yogurt. **Calories per serving 192**

squash, carrot & mango tagine

Calories per serving **232**
  (not including couscous)
Serves **4**
Preparation time **15 minutes**
Cooking time **35–40 minutes**

2 tablespoons **olive oil**
1 large **onion**, cut into large
  chunks
3 **garlic cloves**, finely chopped
1 **butternut squash**, about
  875 g (1¾ lb) in total,
  peeled, deseeded and cubed
2 small **carrots**, peeled and
  cut into thick batons
1 cm (½ inch) **cinnamon stick**
½ teaspoon **turmeric**
¼ teaspoon **cayenne pepper**
  (optional)
½ teaspoon **ground cumin**
1 teaspoon **paprika**
pinch of **saffron** threads
1 tablespoon **tomato purée**
750 ml (1¼ pints) hot
  vegetable stock
1 **mango**, peeled, stoned
  and cut into 2.5 cm (1 inch)
  chunks
salt and **pepper**
2 tablespoons chopped
  coriander, to garnish

Heat the oil in a large, heavy-based saucepan over a medium heat, add the onion and cook for 5 minutes or until beginning to soften. Add the garlic, butternut squash, carrots and spices and fry gently for a further 5 minutes.

Stir in the tomato purée, then pour in the stock and season with salt and pepper to taste. Cover and simmer gently for 20–25 minutes or until the vegetables are tender. Stir in the mango and simmer gently for a further 5 minutes.

Ladle the tagine into serving bowls, sprinkle with the coriander and serve with steamed couscous, if liked.

For spicy squash & carrot soup, make the tagine as above, adding an extra 250 ml (8 fl oz) vegetable stock. Once the vegetables are tender, place in a blender or food processor and blend until smooth. Ladle into bowls and serve scattered with the chopped coriander. **Calories per serving 237**

aubergine & sweet potato wedges

Calories per serving **238**
Serves **4**
Preparation time **15 minutes**
Cooking time **1 hour**

2 large **aubergines**, about
  375 g (12 oz) each
4 tablespoons **brown miso
  paste**
850 ml (1 ½ pints) **boiling
  water**
2 tablespoons **sunflower oil**
5 cm (2 inch) piece of **fresh
  root ginger**, grated
2 **garlic cloves**, crushed
625 g (1 ¼ lb) **sweet
  potatoes**, cut into wedges
12 **spring onions**, thickly
  sliced diagonally
bunch of **parsley**, chopped
salt

Peel the aubergines using a potato peeler and roughly spread the miso paste over the flesh, then place in 2 medium roasting tins. Pour 250 ml (8 fl oz) of the measurement water into each tin, then add 1 tablespoon of the oil, the ginger and garlic. Sprinkle with salt.

Place the sweet potatoes in a separate roasting tin and drizzle with the remaining oil.

Roast the aubergines and sweet potatoes in a preheated oven, 180°C (350°F), Gas Mark 4, for 30 minutes, then pour 125 ml (4 fl oz) of the measurement water into each aubergine tin and roast for a further 20 minutes. Repeat, adding another 50 ml (2 fl oz) measurement water to each aubergine tin, divide the spring onions between them and roast for a further 10 minutes until the aubergine is soft in the centre and the sweet potatoes are tender.

Sprinkle the sweet potatoes with the chopped parsley and cut the aubergines into thick 'steaks'. Serve the aubergines on top of the sweet potatoes with the miso juice from the tins drizzled over.

scallops wrapped in parma ham

Calories per serving **232**
Serves **4**
Preparation time **15 minutes**
Cooking time **4 minutes**

6 slices of **Parma ham**
12 cleaned **king scallops**,
   corals removed (optional)
4 long **rosemary sprigs**
1 tablespoon **olive oil**
green salad leaves
salt and **pepper**

Dressing
4 tablespoons **lemon juice**,
   plus extra to serve
1 **garlic clove**, crushed
1 tablespoon **white wine**
   vinegar
3 tablespoons **olive oil**
1 teaspoon **Dijon mustard**

Cut the slices of Parma ham in half horizontally. Wrap half a slice around the outside of each scallop.

Thread 3 of the scallops on to a metal skewer, alternating with the corals, if using. Once the holes have been made in each scallop, remove the metal skewers and strip the rosemary sprigs of their leaves, leaving just a tuft at the end. Thread the scallops on to the rosemary skewers.

Season the scallops with pepper only. Drizzle the scallops with the oil and cook on a hot barbecue for 2 minutes on each side until cooked through.

Place the dressing ingredients in a bowl and whisk together. Season to taste with salt and pepper. Use to dress the salad leaves and serve with the scallops, seasoned with a squeeze of lemon juice.

For scallop, chorizo & red pepper skewers, thread 1 chopped 10 g (⅓ oz) slice of chorizo sausage, 1 red pepper, cored, deseeded and cut into chunks, and 2 cleaned scallops on to each of 4 presoaked bamboo skewers. Season with salt and pepper, then place on a hot barbecue for 5 minutes, turning occasionally, until the chorizo and scallops are cooked. Serve with the dressed salad as above. **Calories per serving 238**

onion bhajis

Calories per serving **236**
Serves **4**
Preparation time **10 minutes**
Cooking time **6–8 minutes**

225 g (7½ oz) **onions**, thinly
   sliced
115 g (4 oz) **gram flour**
2 teaspoons **cumin seeds**
1 teaspoon **ground coriander**
½ teaspoon **turmeric**
1 **green chilli**, deseeded and
   finely chopped
8 tablespoons **water**
vegetable oil, for frying

Mix together all the ingredients except the water and oil in a bowl. Stir in enough of the measurement water to bind the ingredients together and make a thick batter.

Half-fill a deep saucepan with vegetable oil and heat to 180–190°C (350–375°F), or until a cube of bread browns in 30 seconds. Carefully lower tablespoons of the mixture into the oil, in batches if necessary, and cook for 3–4 minutes, turning until all sides are golden. Remove with a slotted spoon and drain on kitchen paper.

For onion soup, heat 1 tablespoon olive oil and 20 g (¾ oz) butter in a saucepan, add 675 g (1½ lb) sliced onions, then cover with a piece of greaseproof paper and cook over a low heat for 40 minutes until they are dark – do not let them stick. Pour in 125 ml (4 fl oz) red wine and bring to the boil. Stir in 2 tablespoons gram flour and 1.5 litres (2½ pints) beef stock, season well and simmer for 30 minutes. **Calories per serving 195**

poached eggs & spinach

Calories per serving **217 (not including butter)**
Serves **4**
Preparation time **5 minutes**
Cooking time **8–10 minutes**

2 tablespoons **balsamic vinegar**
4 strips of **cherry tomatoes** on the vine, about 6 tomatoes on each
small bunch of **basil**, leaves only
1 tablespoon **distilled vinegar**
4 large **eggs**
4 thick slices of **wholemeal bread**
100 g (3½ oz) **baby leaf spinach**
salt and **pepper**

Pour the balsamic vinegar into a small pan and bubble until reduced by half and it forms syrupy glaze. Set aside.

Lay the cherry tomato vines in an ovenproof dish, drizzle with the balsamic glaze, scatter with the basil leaves and season with salt and pepper. Place in a preheated oven, 180°C (350°F), Gas Mark 4, for 8–10 minutes, or until the tomatoes begin to collapse.

Meanwhile, bring a large saucepan of water to a gentle simmer, add the distilled vinegar and stir with a large spoon to create a swirl. Carefully break 2 eggs into the water and cook for 3 minutes. Remove with a slotted spoon and keep warm. Repeat with the remaining eggs.

Toast the wholemeal bread and butter lightly, if liked.

Heap the spinach on to 4 serving plates and top each plate with a poached egg. Arrange the vine tomatoes on the plates, drizzled with any cooking juices. Serve immediately with the wholemeal toast, cut into fingers.

For spinach, egg & cress salad, gently lower the unshelled eggs into a saucepan of simmering water. Cook for 7–8 minutes, then cool quickly under cold running water. Mix together 2 tablespoons olive oil and 2 tablespoons balsamic vinegar in a small bowl. Shell the eggs and slice thickly. Arrange the egg slices over the baby spinach leaves and halved cherry tomatoes. Scatter with 20 g (¾ oz) salad cress and drizzle with the dressing. Serve immediately. **Calories per serving 210**

red bream with tomato salad

Calories per serving **299**
Serves **4**
Preparation time **15 minutes**
Cooking time **10–12 minutes**

3 tablespoons **olive oil**
4 tablespoons chopped
   coriander
2 **garlic cloves**, crushed
1 teaspoon **coriander seeds**,
   crushed
juice of ½ **lemon**
1 **green chilli**, deseeded and
   finely diced
4 **red bream fillets**, about
   150 g (5 oz) each

Tomato salad
1 tablespoon **walnuts**
4 **plum tomatoes**, chopped
1 tablespoon **olive oil**
1 tablespoon chopped
   coriander

Heat a nonstick frying pan over a medium-low heat and dry-fry the walnuts for 3–4 minutes, stirring frequently, until golden and toasted. Set aside.

Make the spicy dressing for the fish. Mix together the oil, chopped coriander, garlic, coriander seeds, lemon juice and chilli in a bowl, then brush the spice mixture over both sides of the fish fillets.

Line a baking sheet with foil and place the fillets, skin side down, on the foil. Cook under a preheated hot grill for 3–4 minutes on each side until cooked through.

Meanwhile, make the tomato salad. Mix together the tomatoes, toasted walnuts, oil and chopped coriander in a bowl.

Serve the fish with the tomato salad.

For whole baked sea bream, divide 4 chopped garlic cloves, 2 sliced red chillies, 1 trimmed, cleaned and sliced leek, 4 tablespoons chopped parsley and 2 sliced lemons between the cavities of 2 gutted and cleaned whole sea bream. Place in a large baking tray and drizzle with 200 ml (7 fl oz) white wine and 50 ml (2 fl oz) olive oil. Cover with foil and place in a preheated oven, 200°C (400°F), Gas Mark 6, for 10–15 minutes until the fish are cooked through. Divide the fish between 4 plates and serve with steamed green vegetables. **Calories per serving 258**

chilli beef with spring onions

Calories per serving **213**
Serves **4**
Preparation time **10 minutes**
Cooking time **15 minutes**

3 tablespoons **no added sugar oyster sauce**
2 tablespoons **no added sugar Shaoxing rice wine**
2 teaspoons **dried chilli flakes** or 2 **dried red chillies**, halved
100 ml (3½ fl oz) **beef stock**, cooled
1 teaspoon **clear honey**
1 tablespoon **cornflour**
low-calorie **cooking spray**
500 g (1 lb) lean **rump steak**, very thinly sliced
12 **spring onions**, diagonally cut into 3.5 cm (1½ inch) pieces

Mix together the oyster sauce, rice wine, chilli, stock, honey and cornflour in a small bowl until smooth.

Spray a large nonstick wok or frying pan with cooking spray and heat over a high heat until smoking hot.

Add the steak and stir-fry for 3–4 minutes until browned and sealed. Stir in the oyster sauce mixture, then add the spring onions and continue cooking, stirring frequently, for 10 minutes, or until the steak is tender.

For chicken, chilli & vegetable stir-fry, follow the recipe above, replacing the beef with 500 g (1 lb) mini chicken fillets, cut in half lengthways, and adding 1 small finely julienned carrot and 100 g (3½ oz) mangetout, thinly sliced lengthways, instead of the spring onions. **Calories per serving 202**

harissa chicken with tabbouleh

Calories per serving **281**
Serves **4**
Preparation time **10 minutes**
Cooking time **25–30 minutes**

4 **boneless, skinless chicken
  breasts**, about 150 g (5 oz)
  each
2 teaspoons **no added
  sugar harissa paste** (for
  homemade see 202)
1 teaspoon **olive oil**
1 teaspoon **dried oregano**
250 g (8 oz) **cherry tomatoes**
75 g (3 oz) **pitted black olives**
75 g (3 oz) **quinoa**
bunch of **parsley**, chopped
bunch of **coriander**, chopped
bunch of **mint**, chopped
1 **preserved lemon**, diced

Place the chicken breasts in a roasting tin. Mix together the harissa, oil and oregano in a bowl, then rub the mixture all over the chicken breasts.

Cover with foil and roast in a preheated oven, 200°C (400°F), Gas Mark 6, for 15–16 minutes. Remove the foil, add the tomatoes and olives and return to the oven for a further 10–12 minutes, or until the chicken is cooked through.

Meanwhile, cook the quinoa in a saucepan of boiling water according to the packet instructions, then drain and mix with the chopped herbs and preserved lemon.

Slice the chicken and serve with the tabbouleh, the tomatoes and olives and any juices from the tin.

For harissa chicken soup, heat 1 tablespoon olive oil in a frying pan, add 1 chopped onion, 2 peeled and chopped carrots and 1 chopped garlic clove and cook for 4–5 minutes until softened. Stir in 3 teaspoons harissa paste (see above) and cook for a further 1 minute. Stir in a 400 g (13 oz) can chopped tomatoes, a rinsed and drained 400 g (13 oz) can chickpeas and 1 litre (1¾ pints) chicken stock. Bring to the boil, then reduce the heat and simmer for 15 minutes. Stir in 100 g (3½ oz) shredded ready-cooked chicken and 50 g (2 oz) chopped ready-to-eat dried apricots and cook for 10 minutes. Serve sprinkled with 1 tablespoon chopped parsley. **Calories per serving 232**

spicy tofu & vegetable stir-fry

Calories per serving **293 (not including rice)**
Serves **4**
Preparation time **10 minutes**
Cooking time **6 minutes**

4 tablespoons **vegetable oil**
6 **spring onions**, finely sliced
2 **red chillies**, thinly sliced
2.5 cm (1 in) piece of **fresh root ginger**, peeled and finely chopped
4 **garlic cloves**, finely sliced
1 teaspoon crushed **Szechuan peppercorns**
250 g (8 oz) **firm tofu**, cut into 2.5 cm (1 in) cubes
200 g (7 oz) **mangetout**, halved
150 g (5 oz) **baby sweetcorn**, halved lengthways
250 g (8 oz) **pak choi**, chopped
300 g (10 oz) **bean sprouts**
2 tablespoons **light soy sauce**
2 tablespoons **no added sugar Shaoxing rice wine**
4 teaspoons **sesame oil**
salt

Heat 2 tablespoons of the vegetable oil in a wok or deep frying pan, add the spring onions, chillies, ginger, garlic, peppercorns and a pinch of salt. Fry for 1 minute, then add the tofu and stir-fry for a further 2 minutes. Transfer to a plate.

Heat the remaining vegetable oil in the pan and stir-fry the mangetout, sweetcorn, pak choi and bean sprouts for a few minutes, until starting to wilt, then add the soy sauce and rice wine.

Return the tofu mixture to the wok or pan and toss everything together. Drizzle with the sesame oil and serve with brown rice, if liked.

thai steamed fish

Calories per serving **213**
Serves **4**
Preparation time **15 minutes**
Cooking time **15 minutes**

4 **trout fillets**, about 150 g
    (5 oz) each
5 cm (2 inch) piece of **fresh
    root ginger**, peeled and
    chopped
2 **garlic cloves**, chopped
2 **red chillies**, deseeded and
    finely chopped
8 **spring onions**, sliced
grated rind and juice of 2
    limes
4 **pak choi**, quartered
4 tablespoons **soy sauce**

Lay 2 pieces of large foil on a work surface. Place
2 trout fillets on each piece of foil, then divide the
ginger, garlic, chillies, spring onions and lime rind
between them. Drizzle over the lime juice.

Scatter the pak choi around and on top of the fish,
then pour over the soy sauce. Loosely seal the foil
to form parcels, leaving enough space for steam to
circulate as the fish cooks.

Transfer the parcels to a steamer and cook for
15 minutes, or until the fish is cooked through.

Open the parcels carefully, then serve the fish and
pak choi drizzled with the juices.

For Thai fish curry, cook 1 tablespoon no added
sugar red Thai curry paste in a wok for 1 minute, add
1 sliced onion and cook for 4–5 minutes until softened.
Pour in a 400 ml (14 fl oz) can coconut milk and bring
to the boil, then add 500 g (1 lb) skinless salmon
fillets, cut into chunks, and 200 g (7 oz) trimmed and
chopped green beans, reduce the heat and simmer for
5 minutes until the fish is cooked and the beans are
tender. Scatter with 1 tablespoon chopped coriander
and serve with brown rice, if liked. **Calories per
serving 448 (not including rice)**

wasabi beef with garlic pak choi

Calories per serving **295**
Serves **4**
Preparation time **10 minutes**
Cooking time **10–12 minutes**

1 tablespoon **sesame seeds**
2 tablespoons **olive oil**
2 teaspoons **no added sugar wasabi paste**
4 **sirloin steaks**, about 150 g (5 oz) each
200 g (7 oz) **pak choi**, cut lengthways into 8 pieces
5 **garlic cloves**, finely chopped
½ **red chilli**, deseeded and finely diced
1 tablespoon **soy sauce**

Heat a nonstick frying pan over a medium-low heat and dry-fry the sesame seeds for 2 minutes, stirring frequently, until golden brown and toasted. Set aside.

Mix 1 tablespoon of the oil with the wasabi paste in a small bowl, then brush over the steaks.

Heat a griddle pan to very hot, add the steaks and cook for 3–4 minutes on each side depending on how rare you like your steak. Leave to rest for 5 minutes.

Meanwhile, toss the pak choi in the remaining oil with the garlic, chilli and soy sauce, then cook in the griddle pan for 2–3 minutes until wilted.

Slice the steaks, then serve with the pak choi, sprinkled with the toasted sesame seeds.

For beef & pak choi stir-fry, heat 1 tablespoon sunflower oil in a wok or frying pan and cook 300 g (10 oz) sliced sirloin steak for 3–4 minutes until browned, then remove from the pan. Add 300 g (10 oz) broccoli florets, 300 g (10 oz) sugar snap peas, 4 sliced spring onions, 2 chopped garlic cloves, 20 g (¾ oz) peeled and chopped fresh root ginger, 3 quartered pak choi and a splash of water to the pan and stir-fry for 6–7 minutes until the vegetables soften. Return the beef to the pan and heat through. Serve with a sprinkling of soy sauce. **Calories per serving 203**

piri piri swordfish with tomato salsa

Calories per serving **294**
Serves **4**
Preparation time **10 minutes,
    plus marinating**
Cooking time **11–16 minutes**

2 tablespoons **no added
    sugar piri piri seasoning**
2 tablespoons **olive oil**
4 **swordfish steaks**, about
    200 g (7 oz) each
6 ripe **plum tomatoes**, halved
1 tablespoon finely chopped
    parsley
1 tablespoon finely chopped
    basil
1 **green chilli**, deseeded and
    finely chopped
grated rind of 1 **lemon**, plus a
    little juice
salt and **pepper**
lemon wedges, to serve

Mix the piri piri seasoning with 1 tablespoon of the oil and rub it over the swordfish steaks. Cover and leave to marinate in the refrigerator for 30 minutes.

Place the tomatoes on a hot barbecue and cook for about 5–8 minutes until blackened slightly and soft. Leave to cool slightly, then roughly chop and transfer to a bowl. Stir in the parsley, basil, chilli and lemon rind. Add a little lemon juice and the remaining oil and season with salt and pepper.

Cook the marinated swordfish on the barbecue for 3–4 minutes on each side, or until cooked through. Serve with the tomato salsa and lemon wedges.

For barbecued pepper relish, to serve as an alternative accompaniment, core, deseed and chop 1 red, 1 yellow and 1 orange pepper into large chunks. Rub the peppers with 1 tablespoon olive oil mixed with 1 tablespoon no added sugar piri piri seasoning. Place the peppers on a hot barbecue and cook until they have blackened slightly and become really soft, then remove, chop the chunks into smaller pieces and mix with 2 tablespoons olive oil, a little lime juice, 1 tablespoon chopped coriander and 1 deseeded and finely chopped red chilli. Season with salt and pepper.
Calories per serving 128

prune & oat loaf

Calories per slice **251**
Makes **10 slices**
Preparation time **10 minutes**
Cooking time **40–45 minutes**

50 g (2 oz) **coconut oil**,
grated or finely chopped,
plus extra for greasing
275 g (9 oz) **pitted prunes**,
chopped
100 g (3 ½ oz) **rolled oats**
1 ½ teaspoons **bicarbonate
of soda**
125 ml (4 fl oz) **boiling water**
2 **eggs**
150 g (5 oz) good-flavoured
clear honey
175 g (6 oz) **wholemeal flour**
¼ teaspoon **ground
cinnamon**

Grease a 1 kg (2 lb) loaf tin with coconut oil and
line the base with nonstick baking paper.

Place the prunes, oats, bicarbonate of soda and
coconut oil in a heatproof bowl, pour over the
measurement water and leave to stand.

Meanwhile, whisk together the eggs and honey in
a separate bowl until well combined, then fold in the
flour and cinnamon. Add the prune and oat mixture
and mix well.

Spoon the mixture into the prepared tin and bake
in a preheated oven, 180°C (350°F), Gas Mark 4, for
40–45 minutes until a skewer inserted in the centre
comes out clean. Cover the top with foil if it starts to
brown too quickly.

Turn out on to a wire rack and leave to cool, before
cutting into 10 slices to serve.

For prune & cinnamon porridge, place 200 g (7 oz)
rolled oats, 100 g (3½ oz) chopped pitted prunes,
¼ teaspoon ground cinnamon, 1 tablespoon coconut
oil and 1.5 litres (2½ pints) milk or water in a saucepan
and bring to the boil, then reduce the heat and simmer
for 4–5 minutes, stirring occasionally, until thick and
creamy. To serve, pour into 6 bowls and drizzle each
with 1 tablespoon honey. **Calories per serving 373**

cheesy herby muffins

Calories per muffin **281**
Makes **8**
Preparation time **5 minutes**
Cooking time **20 minutes**

175 g (6 oz) **Gruyère cheese**, grated
3 **spring onions**, finely sliced
1 teaspoon **thyme leaves**
1 tablespoon chopped **parsley**
100 g (3½ oz) **rice flour**
½ teaspoon **gluten-free baking powder**
150 g (5 oz) **fresh gluten-free breadcrumbs**
1 teaspoon **no added sugar English mustard**
3 **eggs**, beaten
50 g (2 oz) **butter**, melted
4 tablespoons **milk**

Line 8 holes of a muffin tin with paper muffin cases.

Mix together all the ingredients in a large bowl until just combined and spoon the mixture into the muffin cases.

Place in a preheated oven, 190°C (375°F), Gas Mark 5, for 20 minutes, or until golden and just firm to the touch. Remove from the oven and serve warm.

brazil chocolate brownies

Calories per brownie **289**
Makes **12**
Preparation time **10 minutes,
plus cooling**
Cooking time **40–45 minutes**

100 g (3½ oz) **coconut oil**,
plus extra for greasing
125 g (4 oz) **plain dark no
added sugar chocolate**,
broken into pieces
100 ml (3½ oz) **milk**
175 g (6 oz) **honey**
50 g (2 oz) **cocoa powder**
3 **eggs**
150 g (5 oz) **wholemeal spelt
flour**
1 teaspoon **baking powder**
30 g (3¼ oz) **Brazil nuts**,
roughly chopped

Grease a 18 x 18 cm (7 x 7 inch) baking tin and line
with nonstick baking paper.

Place the coconut oil, chocolate, milk and honey in a
saucepan and heat very gently, stirring, until melted.
Remove from the heat and stir in the cocoa powder,
then leave to cool for a few minutes.

Beat in the eggs, then fold in the flour, baking powder
and Brazil nuts. Pour the mixture into the prepared tin.

Bake in a preheated oven, 190°C (375°F), Gas Mark 5,
for 35–40 minutes until just set. Leave to cool in the tin
for 15 minutes, then transfer to a wire rack and leave to
cool completely. Cut into 12 squares to serve.

For chocolate avocado mousse, place the flesh
of 2 large avocados, 2 tablespoons cocoa powder,
3 tablespoons maple syrup, 2 tablespoons coconut
cream in a food processor or blender and blend until
smooth. Add 150 g (5 oz) melted plain dark no added
sugar chocolate and blend again. Spoon into 4 small
bowls or glasses and serve with fresh raspberries.
Calories per serving 434

summer smoothie

Calories per serving **276**
Serves **1**
Preparation time **5 minutes,
  plus soaking**

1 tablespoon **goji berries**
3 **pitted dates**
2 tablespoons **almond milk**
100 g (3½ oz) **raspberries**,
  plus extra to decorate
75 g (3 oz) **strawberries**,
  hulled
1 tablespoon **clear honey**
3 tablespoons **natural yogurt**
100 ml (3½ fl oz) **coconut
  water**

Place the goji berries and dates in a bowl, pour over the almond milk and leave to soak in the refrigerator for 3 hours, or preferably overnight.

Transfer the goji berry mixture to a blender or food processor, add all the remaining ingredients and blend until smooth, adding a little more coconut water to loosen if needed.

Pour into a glass, decorate with a few extra raspberries and serve.

For summer fruit dessert, toss together 75 g (3 oz) hulled and halved strawberries, 50 g (2 oz) raspberries, 50 g (2 oz) blueberries and 2 tablespoons chopped mint in a serving bowl. Serve with 40 g (1½ oz) natural yogurt. **Calories per serving 90**

tropical fruit desserts

Calories per serving **280**
Serves **4**
Preparation time **15 minutes**

4 **bananas**, sliced
grated rind and juice of 1
   orange
700 g (1½ lb) **natural yogurt**
2 **mangoes**, peeled, stoned
   and chopped
6 **passion fruit**, halved

Place the bananas in a large bowl and toss with the orange rind and juice. Spoon into 4 glasses or bowls.

Top with half the yogurt, then add the mango chunks. Divide the remaining yogurt evenly between the glasses.

Spoon over the pulp of the passion fruit and serve.

For banana splits, bake 4 unpeeled bananas in a preheated oven, 200°C (400°F), Gas Mark 6, for 30 minutes until the skins are black. Halve lengthways and top each one with 1 tablespoon natural yogurt, 1 tablespoon chopped pistachios and a drizzle of honey. **Calories per serving 250**

pancakes with fruit compote

Calories per serving **268**
Serves **4**
Preparation time **10 minutes,
  plus chilling**
Cooking time **20 minutes**

100 g (3½ oz) **buckwheat
  flour**, sifted
½ teaspoon **ground
  cinnamon**
1 large **egg**, beaten
150 ml (¼ pint) **milk**
2 teaspoons **vegetable oil**
4 tablespoons **natural yogurt**,
  to serve

Compote
2 **dessert apples**, peeled,
  cored and chopped
2 **pears**, peeled, cored and
  chopped
100 g (3½ oz) **blueberries**
grated rind and juice of 1
  orange
2–3 tablespoons **water**

Place the flour and half the cinnamon in a bowl and make a well in the centre. Gradually whisk in the egg and milk to form a smooth batter. Chill for 30 minutes.

Heat a little of the oil in a frying pan and pour a ladleful of the batter into the pan, swirling it around to cover the base. Cook until bubbles appear on the surface, then loosen the edges and turn over with a palette knife or spatula and cook for a further 1 minute until golden. Remove from the pan and keep warm. Repeat with the remaining oil and batter to make 8 pancakes.

Meanwhile, make the fruit compote. Place all the ingredients in a small saucepan and simmer for 10 minutes until softened. Keep warm.

Serve the pancakes with the fruit compote, topped with yogurt and sprinkled with the remaining cinnamon.

For cinnamon fruit salad, mix together 2 peeled, cored and chopped dessert apples and 2 peeled, cored and chopped pears in a bowl with 100 g (3½ oz) blueberries, 1 peeled, stoned and chopped mango and 2 peeled and sliced kiwifruit. Pour the juice of 2 oranges over the fruit, sprinkle with 1 teaspoon ground cinnamon and toss together. Leave to stand for 20–30 minutes. Spoon into 4 bowls and serve each with 1 tablespoon natural yogurt. **Calories per serving 168**

green fruit salad

Calories per serving **262**
Serves **6**
Preparation time **15 minutes**

300 g (10 oz) **seedless green grapes**, halved
4 **kiwifruit**, peeled, quartered and sliced
2 ripe **pears**, peeled, cored and sliced
4 **passion fruit**, halved
4 tablespoons **concentrated no added sugar elderflower cordial**
4 tablespoons **water**
300 g (10 oz) **Greek yogurt**
2 tablespoons **clear honey**

Put the grapes, kiwifruit and pears in a bowl. Using a teaspoon, scoop the seeds from 3 of the passion fruit into the bowl. Mix 2 tablespoons of the cordial with the measurement water and drizzle over the salad. Gently toss together and spoon into 6 glasses.

Stir the remaining undiluted cordial into the yogurt, then mix in the honey. Spoon into the glasses. Decorate with the remaining passion fruit seeds and serve.

For ruby fruit salad, mix 300 g (10 oz) halved seedless red grapes with 150 g (5 oz) fresh raspberries and 150 g (5 oz) sliced strawberries. Sprinkle with the seeds from ½ pomegranate, then drizzle with 6 tablespoons no added sugar red grape juice. Mix the yogurt with honey only, then spoon over the fruit salad. Decorate with a few extra pomegranate seeds. **Calories per serving 209**

baked stuffed pears

Calories per serving **217**
Serves **4**
Preparation time **10 minutes**
Cooking time **35–40 minutes**

4 **pears**, halved and cored
100 g (3½ oz) **pitted dates**,
  chopped
1 tablespoon **sesame seeds**
½ teaspoon **ground
  cinnamon**
2 tablespoons **maple syrup**
grated rind and juice of 1
  orange
4 tablespoons **natural yogurt**

Place one half of each of the pears in an ovenproof dish and sprinkle each one with the dates, sesame seeds, cinnamon, maple syrup and orange juice.

Top with the remaining pear halves, cover the dish with foil and bake in a preheated oven, 180°C (350°F), Gas Mark 4, for 35–40 minutes until the pears are tender.

Stir together the orange rind and yogurt in a small bowl, then serve with the baked pears.

For sticky chocolate pears, halve 4 pears, scoop out the cores and place in a baking tin. Sprinkle each half with ¼ tablespoon cocoa nibs, ½ teaspoon honey and 1 teaspoon ground almonds. Squeeze over the juice of 1 orange, cover with foil and cook as above for 30 minutes, or until tender. **Calories per serving 267**

recipes
under 400
calories

butternut & parma ham salad

Calories per serving **372**
Serves **4**
Preparation time **10 minutes**
Cooking time **27 minutes**

1 kg (2 lb) **butternut squash**,
  peeled, deseeded and cut
  into chunks
2 **red onions**, cut into wedges
2 tablespoons **pumpkin
  seeds**
1 tablespoon **olive oil**
175 g (6 oz) **asparagus tips**
12 slices of **Parma ham**
2 tablespoons **extra virgin
  olive oil**
1 tablespoon **balsamic
  vinegar**
2 **chicory bulbs**, leaves
  separated
salt and **pepper**

Place the butternut squash and onions in a roasting tin, sprinkle in the pumpkin seeds and toss with the olive oil and some salt and pepper.

Roast in a preheated oven, 200°C (400°F), Gas Mark 6, for 22 minutes until starting to caramelize, then toss in the asparagus tips and roast for a further 5 minutes.

Meanwhile, place the Parma ham under a preheated hot grill for 4–5 minutes until crisp.

Make the dressing. Whisk together the extra virgin olive oil and vinegar in a small bowl.

Divide the chicory leaves between 4 plates and top with the roasted vegetables and Parma ham. Drizzle with the dressing and serve.

griddled summer chicken salad

Calories per serving **365**
Serves **4**
Preparation time **15 minutes**
Cooking time **40–45 minutes**

4 **boneless, skinless chicken
 breasts**, about 125 g (4 oz)
 each
2 small **red onions**
2 **red peppers**, cored,
 deseeded and cut into flat
 pieces
bunch of **asparagus**, about
 150 g (5 oz), trimmed
200 g (7 oz) **cooked new
 potatoes**, halved
bunch of **basil**
5 tablespoons **olive oil**
2 tablespoons **balsamic
 vinegar**
salt and **pepper**

Heat a griddle pan or frying pan, add the chicken
breasts and cook for 8–10 minutes on each side
until cooked through. Remove from the pan and cut
into chunks.

Cut the red onions into wedges, keeping the root ends
intact to hold the wedges together. Place in the pan
and cook for 5 minutes on each side. Remove from the
pan and set aside.

Place the flat pieces of red pepper in the pan and
cook for 8 minutes on the skin side only, so that the
skins are charred and blistered. Remove and set aside,
then cook the asparagus in the pan for 6 minutes,
turning frequently.

Put the cooked potatoes in a large bowl. Tear the basil,
reserving a few leaves for garnish, and add to the bowl,
together with the chicken and all the vegetables. Add
the olive oil, balsamic vinegar and seasoning. Toss the
salad and garnish with the reserved basil leaves.

For summer chicken wraps, omit the potatoes
and make the recipe as above. Warm 4 soft whole-
wheat tortillas as directed on the packet, then spread
with 175 g (6 oz) reduced-fat hummus. Toss the
griddled chicken, cut into strips, and vegetables with
2 tablespoons olive oil, the balsamic vinegar as above
and reserved basil leaves. Divide between the tortillas,
then roll up tightly and serve cut in half while the
chicken is still warm. **Calories per serving 499**

corn, tomato & black bean salad

Calories per serving **370**
Serves **4**
Preparation time **10 minutes**
Cooking time **10 minutes**

4 **corn cobs**, leaves and fibres
   removed
250 g (8 oz) **cherry tomatoes**,
   halved
400 g (13 oz) can **black
   beans**, rinsed and drained
1 **red onion**, finely diced
1 **avocado**, peeled, stoned
   and diced
small bunch of **coriander**,
   roughly chopped
juice of 1 **lime**
2 tablespoons **rapeseed oil**
2–3 drops of **Tabasco sauce**

Cook the corn cobs in a saucepan of boiling water for 7–10 minutes. Cool briefly under cold running water, then scrape off the kernels with a knife.

Put the kernels in a large bowl with the tomatoes, black beans, onion and avocado and mix with the coriander.

Whisk together the lime juice, oil and Tabasco in a small bowl.

Drizzle the dressing over the salad, stir carefully to combine and serve immediately.

For chilli prawns with corn & black bean salad,
make the salad as above. Heat 1½ tablespoons vegetable oil in a wok or large frying pan over a high heat, add 24 raw peeled and butterflied prawns with the tails on and stir-fry for 1 minute, then add 2 finely chopped garlic cloves and 2 deseeded and finely chopped long red chillies. Fry for a further 2 minutes until the prawns turn pink and are just cooked through. Stir through 3 tablespoons chopped coriander. Serve the prawns on the salad, garnished with extra coriander leaves and lime wedges. **Calories per serving 464**

roasted beetroot soup

Calories per serving **360**
Serves **4**
Preparation time **15 minutes**
Cooking time **1 hour 5 minutes**

600 g (1¼ lb) **raw beetroot**
500 g (1 lb) **potatoes**, peeled and chopped
1 tablespoon **pumpkin seeds**
400 ml (14 fl oz) can **coconut milk**
juice of **1 lemon**
2 teaspoons **ground coriander**
2 teaspoons **dried chilli flakes**
1 teaspoon **ground cumin**
1 **garlic clove**, crushed
salt and **pepper**
2 tablespoons **natural yogurt**, to serve

Place the beetroot in a roasting tin and roast in a preheated oven, 200°C (400°F), Gas Mark 6, for 1 hour until tender. Leave to cool slightly, then peel off the skins.

Meanwhile, cook the potatoes in a saucepan of boiling water for 15–18 minutes until tender.

Heat a nonstick frying pan over a medium-low heat and dry-fry the pumpkin seeds for 2–3 minutes, stirring frequently, until slightly golden and toasted. Set aside.

Transfer the beetroot and potatoes to a blender with the remaining ingredients and blend until smooth. Pour the soup into a saucepan, season to taste and heat through.

Ladle into 4 bowls, sprinkle with the toasted seeds and serve with dollops of yogurt.

For roasted beetroot salad, peel 4 raw beetroot and cut into wedges. Place in a roasting tin with 1 large red onion, cut into wedges, and sprinkle with 1 teaspoon cumin seeds and 1 tablespoon olive oil. Roast as above for 45–50 minutes until the beetroot is tender. Toss together 50 g (2 oz) watercress, 25 g (1 oz) rocket leaves and 40 g (1½ oz) shredded red cabbage in a serving bowl. Add the beetroot, onion, 2 tablespoons extra virgin olive oil and the juice of ½ lemon. Season and toss together. Serve sprinkled with 100 g (3½ oz) grated Manchego cheese and 1 tablespoon chopped coriander. **Calories per serving 246**

beery oxtail & butter bean soup

Calories per serving **310**
Serves **6**
Preparation time **25 minutes**
Cooking time **4¼ hours**

1 tablespoon **sunflower oil**
500 g (1 lb) **oxtail pieces**,
  string removed
1 **onion**, finely chopped
2 **carrots**, peeled and diced
2 **celery sticks**, diced
200 g (7 oz) **potatoes**, peeled
  and diced
small bunch of **mixed herbs**
2 litres (3½ pints) **beef stock**
450 ml (¾ pint) **strong ale**
2 teaspoons **no added sugar
  English mustard**
1 tablespoon **tomato purée**
410 g (13½ oz) can **butter
  beans**, drained
salt and **pepper**
chopped **parsley**, to garnish

Heat the oil in a large saucepan, add the oxtail pieces and fry until browned on one side. Turn the oxtail pieces over and add the onion, stirring until browned on all sides. Stir in the carrots, celery, potatoes and herbs and cook for a further 2–3 minutes.

Pour in the stock and ale, then add the mustard, tomato purée and butter beans. Season well with salt and pepper and bring to the boil, stirring. Half cover the pan and simmer gently for 4 hours.

Lift the oxtail and herbs out of the pan with a slotted spoon. Discard the herbs and cut the meat off the oxtail bones, discarding any fat. Return the meat to the pan and reheat, then taste and adjust the seasoning if needed. Ladle into 6 bowls, sprinkle with chopped parsley and serve.

For chillied oxtail & red bean soup, omit the bunch of mixed herbs and instead stir 2 finely chopped garlic cloves, 2 bay leaves, 1 teaspoon hot chilli powder, 1 teaspoon crushed cumin seeds and 1 teaspoon crushed coriander seeds into the vegetables. Add the beef stock, a 400 g (13 oz) can chopped tomatoes, 1 tablespoon tomato purée and a rinsed and drained 410 g (13½ oz) can red kidney beans. Bring to the boil, simmer and finish as above. **Calories per serving 298**

herby smoked salmon omelettes

Calories per serving **311 (not including baby leaf and herb salad)**
Serves **4**
Preparation time **10 minutes**
Cooking time **15 minutes**

8 large **eggs**
2 **spring onions**, thinly sliced
2 tablespoons chopped **chives**
2 tablespoons chopped **chervil**
50 g (2 oz) **butter**
4 thin slices of **smoked salmon**, cut into thin strips, or 125 g (4 oz) **smoked salmon trimmings**
pepper
baby leaf and herb salad, to serve

Put the eggs, spring onions and herbs in a bowl, beat together lightly and season with pepper.

Heat a medium-sized frying pan over a medium-low heat, add a quarter of the butter and melt until beginning to froth. Pour in a quarter of the egg mixture and swirl to cover the base of the pan. Stir gently for 2–3 minutes or until almost set.

Sprinkle over a quarter of the smoked salmon strips and cook for a further 30 seconds, or until just set. Fold over and slide on to a serving plate. Repeat to make 3 more omelettes. Serve each omelette immediately with baby leaf and herb salad.

For smoked ham & tomato omelette, make as above, adding 8–12 quartered cherry tomatoes to the egg mixture. Replace the smoked salmon with 4 thin slices of smoked ham, cut into strips. **Calories per serving 295**

beef & pak choi stir-fry

Calories per serving **305**
Serves **4**
Preparation time **15 minutes**
Cooking time **5 minutes**

500 g (1 lb) **beef rump steak**,
 trimmed and cut into strips
1 teaspoon **Chinese five-
 spice powder**
2 tablespoons **coconut oil**
1 **red chilli,** deseeded and
 chopped
1 **garlic clove,** chopped
5 cm (2 inch) piece of **fresh
 root ginger,** peeled and cut
 into matchsticks
1 **lemon grass stalk,** trimmed
 and sliced
100 g (3½ oz) **sugar snap peas**
8 **baby corn,** sliced diagonally
6 **spring onions,** sliced
2 **pak choi,** roughly chopped
juice of ½ **lime**
2 tablespoons **soy sauce**
1 tablespoon **no added sugar
 fish sauce**

To garnish
2 tablespoons **roasted
 peanuts**
2 tablespoons roughly
 chopped **coriander**

Toss together the beef strips and five-spice powder
in a bowl, then set aside.

Meanwhile, heat the coconut oil in a wok or large frying
pan, add the chilli, garlic, ginger and lemon grass and
cook for 1 minute until softened. Remove with a slotted
spoon and set aside.

Add the beef to the pan and cook over a high heat for
1 minute until browned and just cooked through. Return
the chilli mixture to the pan with the sugar snaps, baby
corn and spring onions and stir-fry for 1 minute, then
add the pak choi and cook for a further 1 minute.

Pour in the lime juice, soy sauce and fish sauce and
toss well. Spoon on to 4 plates or bowls and serve
sprinkled with the peanuts and chopped coriander.

For Chinese braised beef, heat 2 tablespoons
sunflower oil in a frying pan, add 750 g (1¾ lb) chopped
beef brisket and fry until browned. Set aside. Meanwhile,
put 2 large chopped onions, 50 g (2 oz) peeled fresh
root ginger, 2 garlic cloves and the stalks of a small
bunch of coriander in a food processor or blender and
blitz to a paste. Transfer to a flameproof casserole, add
1 tablespoon water and cook for 2 minutes. Stir in
2 teaspoons Chinese five-spice powder, 4 star anise and
1 teaspoon black peppercorns and cook for 1 minute.
Stir in 2 tablespoons soy sauce, 2 tablespoons tomato
purée and 2 tablespoons maple syrup, add the beef, pour
over enough water to cover and bring to a simmer. Cover
and place in a preheated oven, 170°C (325°F), Gas Mark
3, for 2 hours. Serve with steamed pak choi. **Calories
per serving 226**

crusted salmon with tomato salsa

Calories per serving **353**
Serves **4**
Preparation time **10 minutes**
Cooking time **12–15 minutes**

1 tablespoon chopped **fresh
  herbs**
1 **garlic clove**, crushed
3 tablespoons **polenta**
4 skinless **salmon fillets**,
  about 125 g (4 oz) each
pepper

Salsa
375 g (12 oz) **cherry
  tomatoes**, quartered
1 small **red onion**, finely sliced
½ **red chilli**, deseeded and
  finely chopped
handful of **coriander**, chopped

To serve
4 tablespoons **light crème
  fraîche**
green salad

Mix together the herbs, garlic and polenta in a shallow bowl. Coat the salmon pieces in the polenta mix, pressing it down firmly.

Put the coated fish on a baking sheet and place in a preheated oven, 200°C (400°F), Gas Mark 6, for 12–15 minutes until cooked through.

Mix together the salsa ingredients in a bowl. Place the salmon on 4 serving plates, top with the salsa, season with pepper and serve with a spoonful of crème fraîche and a green salad.

For polenta-crusted chicken, beat together 2 tablespoons cream cheese with the chopped fresh herbs and 1 finely diced garlic clove. Make a horizontal slit in 4 x 125 g (4 oz) boneless, skinless chicken breasts. Fill the cavities of the chicken breasts with the cream cheese mixture, then secure with cocktail sticks. Dip the chicken breasts in a little gluten-free flour, a little beaten egg, then in the polenta. Fry each chicken breast in 1 tablespoon olive oil for 2–3 minutes on each side, transfer to a baking sheet and place in a preheated oven, 200°C (400°F), Gas Mark 6, for 10–12 minutes, or until the chicken is cooked through. Serve with the salsa and a green salad. **Calories per serving 362**

mixed bean & tomato chilli

Calories per serving **377**
Serves **4**
Preparation time **5 minutes**
Cooking time **20–25 minutes**

2 tablespoons **olive oil**
1 **onion**, finely chopped
4 **garlic cloves**, crushed
1 teaspoon **dried chilli flakes**
2 teaspoons **ground cumin**
1 teaspoon **ground cinnamon**
400 g (13 oz) can **chopped tomatoes**
200 ml (7 fl oz) **vegetable stock**
400 g (13 oz) can **mixed beans**, rinsed and drained
400 g (13 oz) can **red kidney beans**, rinsed and drained
salt and **pepper**

To serve
4 tablespoons **soured cream**
25 g (1 oz) finely chopped **coriander**
4 griddled **corn tortillas**

Heat the oil in a heavy-based saucepan, add the onion and garlic and fry for 3–4 minutes until softened, then add the chilli, cumin and cinnamon. Cook, stirring, for 2–3 minutes.

Stir in the tomatoes and stock and bring to the boil, then reduce the heat to medium and simmer gently for 10 minutes. Add the beans and cook for 3–4 minutes until warmed through. Season well.

Ladle into 4 bowls and top each with 1 tablespoon of soured cream. Sprinkle with chopped coriander and serve immediately with the corn tortillas.

For mixed bean, tomato & chilli bruschettas, place ½ onion, 2 crushed garlic cloves, 1 teaspoon dried chilli flakes, 100 g (3½ oz) chopped tomatoes, a rinsed and drained 400 g (13 oz) can mixed beans and 4 tablespoons chopped flat leaf parsley in a blender or food processor and whizz until fairly smooth. Season, then spread the mixture on to 2 halved and toasted ciabatta rolls, drizzle each with 2 teaspoons olive oil and serve. **Calories per serving 259**

spiced yogurt chicken

Calories per serving **319**
Serves **4**
Preparation time **10 minutes,
  plus marinating**
Cooking time **30–35 minutes**

200 g (7 oz) **natural yogurt**
juice of 1 **lemon**
2 **garlic cloves**, crushed
1 tablespoon peeled and
  grated **fresh root ginger**
1 **green chilli**, deseeded and
  finely diced
1 teaspoon **turmeric**
1 teaspoon **paprika**
1 teaspoon **garam masala**
2 tablespoons **olive oil**
4 **boneless, skinless chicken
  breasts**, about 150 g (5 oz)
  each
6 **spring onions**, sliced
300 g (10 oz) **spinach**
pepper
2 tablespoons chopped
  coriander, to garnish
2 tablespoons **toasted flaked
  almonds**, to serve

Mix together the yogurt, lemon juice, garlic, ginger, chilli, spices and 1 tablespoon of the oil in a non-reactive dish. Make a few cuts across the chicken, then place in the marinade, rubbing the mixture into the cuts. Cover and leave to marinate in the refrigerator for 1 hour.

Place the chicken in a baking tray and bake in a preheated oven, 200°C (400°F), Gas Mark 6, for 30–35 minutes until golden and cooked through.

Meanwhile, heat the remaining oil in a pan, add the spring onions and sauté for 3–4 minutes until softened, then add the spinach and toss in the hot oil to wilt. Season with pepper.

Divide the spinach between 4 plates and top each with a chicken breast. Serve sprinkled with the chopped coriander and flaked almonds.

For spicy chicken open sandwiches, mix together 3 tablespoons no added sugar mayonnaise, the juice of ½ lemon and ½ teaspoon smoked paprika in a bowl. Add 300 g (10 oz) shredded ready-cooked chicken and 4 sliced spring onions. Toast 4 thick slices of gluten-free bread, then top each one with 2 Little Gem lettuce leaves and spoon over the chicken mixture. Peel, stone and slice 1 mango and serve a few slices on the top of each sandwich, with a sprinkling of coriander leaves. **Calories per serving 201**

seared tuna with lime crust

Calories per serving **310**
Serves **4**
Preparation time **10 minutes,
  plus marinating**
Cooking time **5 minutes**

4 **tuna steaks**, about 150 g
  (5 oz) each
2 tablespoons grated **lime
  rind**
juice of 3 **limes**
3 tablespoons chopped **dill**
2 tablespoons chopped
  parsley
1 **red chilli**, deseeded and
  finely diced
3 tablespoons **olive oil**
6 **pak choi**, quartered
  lengthways
salt and **pepper**

Place the tuna in a shallow non-reactive dish. Combine the lime rind, juice, dill, parsley, chilli, 2 tablespoons of the oil and salt and pepper in a small bowl, then pour over the tuna. Cover and leave to marinate in the refrigerator for 20 minutes, turning the tuna once.

Remove the tuna from the marinade. Heat the remaining oil in a frying pan or griddle pan and cook the tuna for 1–2 minutes on each side until just seared. Remove from the pan and thickly slice. Pour any remaining marinade into the pan and bring to the boil.

Meanwhile, place the pak choi in a steamer and cook for 3–4 minutes until tender.

Divide the pak choi between 4 plates and top with the sliced tuna. Serve drizzled with the hot marinade.

For tuna salad with lime dressing, whisk together 3 tablespoons olive oil, the juice of 1 lime, 1 teaspoon clear honey and ½ teaspoon Dijon mustard in a small bowl. Cook 350 g (11½ oz) tuna steak on a griddle for 2–3 minutes on each side, then slice. Toss together the leaves of 4 Little Gem lettuces, 12 halved cherry tomatoes, 50 g (2 oz) black olives, a few sprigs of dill and parsley and ½ thinly sliced red onion. Toss in the tuna and dressing and serve. **Calories per serving 249**

roasted fennel pork chops

Calories per serving **396**
Serves **4**
Preparation time **10 minutes**
Cooking time **20 minutes**

4 **pork chops**, about 175 g
(6 oz) each
1 tablespoon **olive oil**
1 teaspoon **fennel seeds**
2 tablespoons **extra virgin
olive oil**
2 tablespoons **red wine
vinegar**
2–3 **sage leaves**, chopped
4 **dessert apples**, cored and
thinly sliced into rings
3 **celery sticks**, thickly sliced
12 **green grapes**, halved
pepper

Brush the chops with the olive oil and sprinkle with the fennel seeds and pepper.

Place on a rack over a roasting tray and bake in a preheated oven, 200°C (400°F), Gas Mark 6, for 20 minutes until cooked through.

Meanwhile, whisk together the extra virgin olive oil, vinegar and sage in a bowl.

Toss the apples, celery and grapes together with the dressing and serve with the roasted chops.

144

coconut fish curry

Calories per serving **399**
Serves **4**
Preparation time **5 minutes**
Cooking time **12–15 minutes**

1 tablespoon **groundnut oil**
2 teaspoons **ground cumin**
2 teaspoons **ground coriander**
2 **green chillies**, deseeded and sliced
1 **cinnamon stick**
1 **star anise**
6 **kaffir lime leaves**
400 ml (14 fl oz) can **light coconut milk**
4 skinless **cod loins**, about 150 g (5 oz) each
juice of 1 **lime**
fresh **coriander leaves**, to garnish (optional)
600 g (1¼ lb) cooked **brown basmati rice**, to serve

Heat the oil in a saucepan, add the spices and lime leaves and cook, stirring, for 2 minutes until fragrant. Pour in the coconut milk and simmer for 5 minutes.

Add the fish and simmer for 4–6 minutes until the fish is tender and cooked through. Stir in the lime juice.

Sprinkle with coriander leaves, if liked, and serve with the basmati rice.

For coconut fish soup, bring 1 litre (1¾ pints) fish stock to a simmer in a saucepan, then add 50 g (2 oz) chopped kale, 50 g (2 oz) sliced mushrooms, 1 sliced red chilli, 350 g (11½ oz) sliced cod loin and 50 g (2 oz) raw peeled prawns. Simmer for 2–3 minutes, then add 200 ml (7 fl oz) coconut cream and simmer for a further 4–5 minutes until the prawns turn pink and the fish is cooked through. Serve sprinkled with coriander leaves. **Calories per serving 174**

lamb with aubergine dressing

Calories per serving **348**

Serves **4**

Preparation time **5 minutes, plus marinating**

Cooking time **18–20 minutes**

12 **lamb cutlets**, about 100 g (3½ oz) each

1 tablespoon **olive oil**

2 **garlic cloves**, crushed

1 teaspoon **sumac** or **ground cumin**

½ teaspoon **dried oregano**

1 **aubergine**

50 g (2 oz) **feta cheese**, crumbled

75 ml (3 fl oz) **natural yogurt**

1 tablespoon **tahini**

juice of 1 **lemon**

50 g (2 oz) **watercress**

Place the lamb cutlets in a bowl with half the oil and garlic, the sumac or cumin and oregano and mix well to coat. Cover and leave to marinate in the refrigerator for 30 minutes.

Meanwhile, cook the aubergine under a preheated hot grill for 10 minutes, turning frequently, until the skin is blackened. Leave to cool, then remove the stalk.

Place the whole aubergine, feta, yogurt, tahini and lemon juice in a food processor or blender and blend until smooth.

Cook the lamb cutlets under a preheated grill for 4–5 minutes on each side, depending on how pink you like your lamb.

Serve the lamb on a bed of watercress with the aubergine dressing.

For spiced lamb burgers, mix together 750 g (1½ lb) minced lamb, 2 chopped garlic cloves, 1 tablespoon chopped mint and 1 teaspoon smoked paprika in a bowl. Shape into 4 burgers, then brush with ½ tablespoon oil and cook under a preheated hot grill or on a barbecue for 5–6 minutes on each side until cooked through. Serve on a bed of 50 g (2 oz) watercress, 50 g (2 oz) spinach and ¼ sliced cucumber dressed with 2 tablespoons no added sugar salad dressing. Crumble over 50 g (2 oz) feta cheese to serve. **Calories per serving 458**

spiced mackerel fillets

Calories per serving **399 (not including rocket salad)**
Serves **4**
Preparation time **15 minutes**
Cooking time **5–6 minutes**

2 tablespoons **olive oil**
1 tablespoon **smoked paprika**
1 teaspoon **cayenne pepper**
4 **mackerel**, scaled, filleted and pin-boned
2 **limes**, quartered
salt and **pepper**

Mix together the oil, paprika and cayenne with a little salt and pepper. Make 3 shallow cuts in the skin of the mackerel and brush over the spiced oil.

Place the lime quarters and mackerel on a hot barbecue, skin side down, and cook for 4–5 minutes until the skin is crispy and the limes are charred. Turn the fish over and cook for a further 1 minute until cooked through. Serve with a rocket salad, if liked.

For mackerel with black pepper & bay, mix together 4 very finely shredded bay leaves, 1 crushed garlic clove, ½ teaspoon pepper, a pinch of salt and 4 tablespoons olive oil. Rub the marinade over and into the cavity of 4 gutted and scaled mackerel. Place them on a very hot barbecue and cook for 3–4 minutes on each side. **Calories per serving 445**

bean, chorizo & spinach stew

Calories per serving **318**
Serves **4**
Preparation time **5 minutes**
Cooking time **25 minutes**

½ tablespoon **olive oil**
125 g (4 oz) **chorizo**, diced
1 **onion**, chopped
2 **garlic cloves**, chopped
2 x 400 g (13 oz) cans **butter beans**, rinsed and drained
400 g (13 oz) can **chopped tomatoes**
600 ml (1 pint) **chicken stock**
200 g (7 oz) **baby spinach leaves**
2 tablespoons chopped **parsley**
salt and **pepper**

Heat the oil in a large pan, add the chorizo and cook for 2–3 minutes. Add the onion and cook over a low heat for a further 10 minutes until soft, then stir in the garlic and cook for a further 1 minute.

Add the butter beans, tomatoes and stock, bring to a gentle simmer, cover and cook for 10 minutes.

Stir in the spinach and half the parsley and cook for 1 minute until the spinach has wilted. Season to taste and serve sprinkled with the remaining parsley.

For butter bean dip, place a rinsed and drained 400 g (13 oz) can butter beans, 2 garlic cloves, the juice of 1 lemon, 2 tablespoons olive oil, 1 teaspoon ground cumin and ½ teaspoon paprika in a food processor or blender and blend until smooth, adding a little water to loosen if necessary. Serve with chopped vegetables.
Calories per serving 107 (not including vegetables)

snapper with carrots & caraway

Calories per serving **352**
Serves **4**
Preparation time **10 minutes**
Cooking time **15 minutes**

500 g (1 lb) **carrots**, sliced
2 teaspoons **caraway seeds**
4 **snapper fillets**, about 175 g
 (6 oz) each, pin-boned
2 **oranges**
bunch of **coriander**, roughly
 chopped, plus extra to
 garnish
4 tablespoons **olive oil**
salt and **pepper**

Heat a griddle pan over a medium heat and cook the carrots for 3 minutes on each side, adding the caraway seeds for the last 2 minutes of cooking. Transfer to a bowl and keep warm.

Cook the snapper fillets in the griddle pan for 3 minutes on each side until cooked through. Meanwhile, juice 1 of the oranges and cut the other into quarters. Cook the orange quarters in the griddle pan until browned.

Add the coriander to the carrots and mix well. Season to taste with salt and pepper and stir in the oil and orange juice. Serve the cooked fish with the carrots and orange quarters. Garnish with extra coriander.

For carrot & coriander purée, to serve as an alternative accompaniment, cook 500 g (1 lb) peeled and roughly chopped carrots in a saucepan of lightly salted boiling water until very soft. Drain, then transfer to a food processor or blender with 2 tablespoons double cream and a little salt and pepper and whizz together until very smooth. Stir in 1 tablespoon finely chopped coriander leaves and serve. **Calories per serving 86**

spinach omelette arnold bennett

Calories per serving **349**
Serves **4**
Preparation time **15 minutes**
Cooking time **20–25 minutes**

350 g (12 oz) **spinach**
350 ml (12 fl oz) **milk**
250 g (8 oz) **smoked haddock**
1 teaspoon **black peppercorns**
40 g (1½ oz) **unsalted butter**
1 tablespoon **rice flour**
5 **eggs**, lightly whisked
25 g (1 oz) **Parmesan cheese**, grated
salt and **pepper**

Place the spinach in a sieve and pour over boiling water until wilted. Set aside.

Put the milk, haddock and peppercorns in a frying pan and bring to a simmer, then cook for 5 minutes until the fish is just cooked through. Lift out the fish using a fish slice and leave to cool. Strain the milk into a jug.

Melt 30 g (1 oz) of the butter in a small saucepan, stir in the flour and cook, stirring, for 1 minute. Add the strained milk a little at a time, stirring continuously, until the sauce is creamy and thick. Simmer for 4–5 minutes.

Remove the skin and any bones from the fish, then flake the flesh into large pieces. Stir the wilted spinach and flaked fish into the sauce and season.

Melt the remaining butter in an ovenproof frying pan, add the eggs and cook for 3–4 minutes until the eggs are still slightly liquid on top. Pour over the sauce, sprinkle with the cheese and cook under a preheated hot grill for 3–4 minutes until golden and bubbling.

For eggs Florentine, place 2 egg yolks in a heatproof bowl over a pan of simmering water and beat for 4–5 minutes. Add ½ tablespoon lemon juice, ½ tablespoon water and a pinch of salt and pepper, then beat for a further 1 minute. Add 100 g (3½ oz) cubed butter, a few cubes at a time, beating continuously, until the sauce is the consistency of double cream. Poach 4 eggs (see page 88). Meanwhile, wilt 400 g (13 oz) spinach as above. Divide the wilted spinach between 2 halved gluten-free wholemeal rolls, then top each one with a poached egg. Pour over the hollandaise sauce and serve. **Calories per serving 395**

lemon & sage dover sole

Calories per serving **319**
Serves **4**
Preparation time **10 minutes**
Cooking time **35–40 minutes**

500 g (1 lb) **new potatoes**,
   scrubbed
a few **rosemary sprigs**
2 tablespoons **olive oil**
2 **Dover soles**, about
   250 g (8 oz) each, filleted
   and pin-boned
grated rind and juice of 1
   lemon
50 ml (2 fl oz) **double cream**
6 **sage leaves**, finely shredded
salt and **pepper**

Cook the new potatoes in a saucepan of salted boiling water for 6–8 minutes until almost tender. Drain and place in an ovenproof dish with the rosemary, drizzle with 1 tablespoon of the oil and season with salt. Roast in a preheated oven, 200°C (400°F), Gas Mark 6, for 20 minutes, or until golden brown. Turn the oven off but leave the potatoes in it to keep warm while you cook the fish.

Heat the remaining oil in a large frying pan. Season the fish with salt and pepper and place it, skin side down, in the hot pan. Cook for 3–4 minutes, or until the skin becomes crispy. Turn the fish over and cook for a further 1 minute. Remove the fish from the pan and keep warm while you make the sauce.

Put the lemon rind and juice, cream and sage into the pan and stir well to combine. Add a little water if the sauce becomes too thick.

Pour the sauce over the fish and serve with the roasted new potatoes.

For pan-fried Dover sole with potato & fennel salad, place 500 g (1 lb) cooked, warm new potatoes in a bowl with 1 finely shredded fennel bulb. Heat 1 tablespoon olive oil in a small frying pan, add 1 tablespoon yellow mustard seeds and cook until they begin to pop. Add these to the potatoes. Make the sauce as above, omitting the sage. Pour over the potatoes and fennel, season and serve with the Dover sole pan-fried as above. **Calories per serving 324**

roast pork loin with creamy veg

Calories per serving **387**
Serves **4**
Preparation time **10 minutes**
Cooking time **25–30 minutes**

1 teaspoon **ground cumin**
1 teaspoon **ground coriander**
500 g (1 lb) **pork loin**,
   trimmed of fat
3 tablespoons **olive oil**
300 g (10 oz) **sweet
   potatoes**, peeled and
   chopped
250 g (8 oz) **Savoy cabbage**,
   shredded
3 **leeks**, trimmed, cleaned and
   sliced
3 tablespoons **soured cream**
2 teaspoons **no added sugar
   wholegrain mustard**

Mix together the spices in a bowl, then rub over the pork. Heat 1 tablespoon of the oil in an ovenproof frying pan, add the pork and cook until browned on all sides. Transfer to a preheated oven, 180°C (350°F), Gas Mark 4, and cook for 20–25 minutes, or until cooked through. Leave to rest for 2 minutes.

Meanwhile, cook the sweet potatoes in a saucepan of boiling water for 12–15 minutes until tender, adding the cabbage and leeks 3–4 minutes before the end of the cooking time. Drain well.

Heat the remaining oil in a frying pan, add the vegetables and fry for 7–8 minutes until starting to turn golden. Stir in the cream and mustard.

Slice the pork and serve on top of the vegetables.

For grilled pork chops with cabbage & leek mash, cook 4 x 150 g (5 oz) pork chops, trimmed of all fat, under a preheated hot grill for 5 minutes on each side, or until cooked through. Meanwhile, cook 500 g (1 lb) peeled and finely diced potatoes, ½ finely shredded Savoy cabbage and 2 trimmed, cleaned and finely sliced leeks in a saucepan of boiling water for 8 minutes until tender. Drain, then mash in the pan with 2 tablespoons natural yogurt and salt and pepper. Serve with the pork. **Calories per serving 324**

cod saltimbocca

Calories per serving **322**
Serves **4**
Preparation time **10 minutes**
Cooking time **10 minutes**

4 skinless **cod loins**, about
   150 g (5 oz) each, halved
   lengthways
8 slices of **prosciutto**
8 **sage leaves**
200 g (7 oz) **frozen peas**
200 g (7 oz) **frozen broad
   beans**
400 g (13 oz) **asparagus**,
   trimmed
1 tablespoon **olive oil**

Wrap each cod loin in a slice of prosciutto, placing a sage leaf under the ends of each one.

Cook the peas, beans and asparagus in a saucepan of simmering water for 4 minutes until tender. Drain and remove the outer skins of the beans, if liked. Set aside.

Heat the oil in a frying pan, add the fish, sage side down, and cook for 3 minutes until the prosciutto is crisp, then turn over and cook for a further 2 minutes until the fish is cooked through. Remove the fish from the pan and keep warm.

Toss the vegetables in the oil in the pan, then transfer to 4 plates and top with the fish.

For prosciutto & figs, halve 8 figs lengthways and cook them cut side down on a griddle for 1 minute, until charred. Sprinkle with 2 tablespoons balsamic vinegar while still warm, then wrap each one with ½ slice of prosciutto. Serve sprinkled with 2 tablespoons Parmesan cheese shavings and a few mint leaves.
Calories per serving 125

wild rice jambalaya

Calories per serving **375 (not including bread)**
Serves **4**
Preparation time **15 minutes**
Cooking time **35 minutes**

125 g (4 oz) **wild rice**
1 teaspoon **olive oil**
50 g (2 oz) **celery**, chopped
½ **red pepper**, cored, deseeded and diced
½ **green** or **yellow pepper**, cored, deseeded and diced
1 **onion**, chopped
1 **rindless lean back bacon rasher**, trimmed of fat
2 **garlic cloves**, crushed
2 tablespoons **tomato purée**
1 tablespoon chopped **thyme**
125 g (4 oz) **long-grain rice**
1 **green chilli**, deseeded and finely chopped
½ teaspoon **cayenne pepper**
400 g (13 oz) can **tomatoes**, drained
300 ml (½ pint) **chicken stock**
150 ml (¼ pint) **dry white wine**
250 g (8 oz) medium **raw peeled prawns**
chopped **parsley**, to garnish

Place the wild rice in a saucepan with water to cover. Bring to the boil and boil for 5 minutes. Remove the pan from the heat and cover tightly. Leave to steam for about 10 minutes until the grains are tender. Drain.

Heat the oil in a large nonstick frying pan. Add the celery, peppers, onion, bacon and garlic. Cook, stirring, for 3–4 minutes until the vegetables are soft. Stir in the tomato purée and thyme. Cook for a further 2 minutes.

Add the wild rice, long-grain rice, chilli, cayenne pepper, tomatoes, stock and wine. Bring to the boil. Reduce the heat and simmer for 10 minutes until the rice is tender but still firm to the bite.

Add the prawns and cook, stirring occasionally, for 5 minutes, until the prawns turn pink and are cooked through. Spoon into 4 bowls. Scatter with parsley and serve with crusty bread, if liked.

For chicken & prawn jambalaya, omit the wild rice and increase the quantity of long-grain rice to 250 g (8 oz). Soften the celery, peppers, onion and garlic as above, omitting the bacon. Remove from the pan and heat 1 tablespoon of olive oil in the same pan. Add 200 g (4 oz) chicken breast, cut into chunks, and fry until golden on all sides. Return the softened vegetables to the pan, then add the remaining ingredients up to and including the white wine. Bring to the boil, then complete the recipe as above. **Calories per serving 396**

pumpkin & goats' cheese bake

Calories per serving **320**
Serves **4**
Preparation time **20 minutes**
Cooking time **25–30 minutes**

400 g (13 oz) **raw beetroot**,
   peeled and diced
625 g (1¼ lb) **pumpkin** or
   butternut squash, peeled,
   deseeded and cut into
   slightly larger dice
1 **red onion**, cut into wedges
2 tablespoons **olive oil**
2 teaspoons **fennel seeds**
2 small **goats' cheeses**, about
   100 g (3½ oz) each
salt and **pepper**
chopped **rosemary**, to garnish

Place the beetroot, pumpkin or squash and onion in a roasting tin, drizzle with the oil and sprinkle with the fennel seeds and salt and pepper. Roast the vegetables in a preheated oven, 200°C (400°F), Gas Mark 6, for 20–25 minutes, turning once, until well browned and tender.

Cut the goats' cheeses in to three and nestle each slice among the roasted vegetables. Sprinkle the cheeses with a little salt and pepper and drizzle with some of the pan juices.

Return the dish to the oven for about 5 minutes, until the cheese is just beginning to melt. Sprinkle with rosemary and serve immediately.

For beetroot & pumpkin penne, roast the vegetables as above for 20–25 minutes, omitting the fennel seeds. Cook 350 g (11½ oz) penne pasta in a saucepan of salted boiling water, then drain, reserving one ladleful of the cooking water. Return the pasta to the pan and add the roasted vegetables, a handful of torn basil leaves and the cooking water. Omit the goats' cheese and rosemary. Place over a high heat, stirring, for 30 seconds and serve. **Calories per serving 485**

pork with pecans & apricots

Calories per serving **396**
Serves **4**
Preparation time **5 minutes**
Cooking time **10–15 minutes**

1 teaspoon **dried sage**
1 tablespoon **olive oil**
600 g (1¼ lb) **pork tenderloin**
75 g (3 oz) **pecan nuts**
8 **apricots**, halved and stoned
4 tablespoons **orange juice**
steamed **green beans**, to
 serve

Mix together the sage and oil, then rub this over the pork before cutting it into thick medallions.

Heat a frying pan, add the pork and cook for 3–4 minutes on each side until golden and cooked through. Remove from the pan and keep warm.

Add the pecans to the pan and cook for 2 minutes until golden. Return the pork to the pan, add the apricots and pour in the orange juice. Bring to the boil, then reduce the heat and simmer for 2–3 minutes.

Serve with steamed green beans.

For pork & apricot burgers, mix together 500 g (1 lb) minced pork, 2 crushed garlic cloves, 1 teaspoon smoked paprika, 1 beaten egg and 6 diced dried apricots in a bowl. Shape into 4 burgers. Heat 1 tablespoon olive oil in a frying pan and cook the burgers for 6–7 minutes on each side until cooked through. Serve with a crisp green salad. **Calories per serving 328**

apricot & almond cake

Calories per serving **318**
Serves **6**
Preparation time **15 minutes,
  plus cooling**
Cooking time **50–55 minutes**

butter, for greasing
150 g (5 oz) **ready-to-eat
  dried apricots**
125 g (4 oz) **sweet potatoes,**
  peeled and chopped
125 ml (4 fl oz) **water**
3 **oranges**
3 **eggs**, separated
90 g (3¼ oz) **ground
  almonds**
90 g (3¼ oz) **rice flour**
1 teaspoon **baking powder**

To serve
300 g (10 oz) **natural yogurt**
¼ teaspoon **ground
  cinnamon**

Grease a 20 cm (8 inch) cake tin with butter and line the base with nonstick baking paper.

Place the apricots in a heatproof bowl, pour over enough boiling water to cover and leave to soak for 1 minute. Drain, then chop three-quarters of the apricots, reserving the rest.

Put the chopped apricots, the sweet potatoes and measurement water in a saucepan and cook over a low heat for 20–25 minutes until the liquid is absorbed and the sweet potatoes and apricots are soft.

Place the cooked sweet potatoes and apricots, the reserved apricots, the grated rind and juice of 1 orange and the egg yolks in a food processor or blender and blend until smooth. Whisk the egg whites in a clean bowl until stiff, then gently fold the apricot mixture into the whites. Fold in the almonds, flour and baking powder.

Spoon the mixture into the prepared tin, level the surface and bake in a preheated oven, 180°C (350°F), Gas Mark 4, for 30 minutes until a skewer inserted into the centre comes out clean. Leave to cool in the tin for 10 minutes.

Meanwhile, heat the juice and rind of the remaining oranges in a small saucepan and boil until reduced and syrupy.

Turn the cake out on to a serving plate and pour over the syrup. Serve hot or cold, cut into 6 slices, with dollops of yogurt sprinkled with ground cinnamon.

maple apple cake

Calories per serving **312**
Serves **8**
Preparation time **10 minutes**
Cooking time **40–45 minutes**

125 g (4 oz) **coconut oil**,
  melted, plus extra for
  greasing
175g (6 oz) **wholemeal flour**
1 teaspoon **baking powder**
½ teaspoon **ground
  cinnamon**
600 g (1¼ lb) **Bramley
  apples**, peeled, cored and
  diced
50 g (2 oz) **sultanas**
75 ml (3 fl oz) **maple syrup**
2 **eggs**

Grease a 20 cm (8 inch) spring-form cake tin with coconut oil and line the base with nonstick baking paper.

Place the flour, baking powder and cinnamon in a bowl and mix well. Stir in the apples and sultanas and mix to coat with the dry ingredients.

Whisk together the maple syrup, eggs and coconut oil in a jug, then pour into the dry ingredients and mix together until well combined.

Spoon the mixture into the prepared cake tin and level the top. Bake in a preheated oven, 180°C (350°F), Gas Mark 4, for 40–45 minutes until a skewer inserted in the centre comes out clean. Transfer to a wire rack and leave to cool. Cut into 8 slices to serve.

For maple apple crisp, place 4 peeled, cored and sliced dessert apples in an ovenproof baking dish. Place 150 g (5 oz) oats, 75 g (3 oz) coconut oil, ½ teaspoon ground cinnamon and 25 g (1 oz) walnut pieces in a food processor and pulse briefly to break down the oats and walnuts. Sprinkle the mixture over the apples, then drizzle with 75 ml (3 fl oz) maple syrup. Bake in a preheated oven, 200°C (400°F), Gas Mark 6, for 15–18 minutes until golden and crisp. Divide between 8 bowls and serve with crème fraîche, if liked. **Calories per serving 235 (not including crème fraîche)**

roasted rhubarb with coconut rice

Calories per serving **324**
Serves **4**
Preparation time **5 minutes**
Cooking time **15 minutes**

1½ tablespoons **honey**
400 g (13 oz) **rhubarb**,
   trimmed and chopped
100 g (3½ oz) **basmati rice**
400 ml (14 fl oz) can **coconut milk**
100 ml (3½ fl oz) **water**
1 tablespoon **toasted flaked almonds**

Heat 1 tablespoon of the honey in a small saucepan. Put the rhubarb in a roasting tin and pour over the honey. Place in a preheated oven, 200°C (400°F), Gas Mark 6, for 10 minutes.

Meanwhile, place the rice, coconut milk, measurement water and remaining honey in a saucepan and bring to a simmer, then cook for 12–15 minutes, stirring occasionally, until the rice is tender.

Serve the rice pudding topped with the roasted rhubarb and sprinkled with a few flaked almonds.

banana & buttermilk pancakes

Calories per serving **315**
Serves **4**
Preparation time **10 minutes**
Cooking time **12–15 minutes**

125 g (4 oz) **plain flour**
1 teaspoon **baking powder**
pinch of **salt**
200 ml (7 fl oz) **buttermilk**
1 **egg**
2 small **bananas**, thinly sliced
1 tablespoon **vegetable oil**

To serve
1 **banana**, sliced
25 g (1 oz) **pecan nuts**,
   chopped
1 tablespoon **clear honey**

Sift the flour, baking powder and salt into a large bowl and make a well in the centre. Whisk together the buttermilk and egg in a jug, then gradually whisk into the flour mixture to form a smooth batter. Stir in the sliced bananas.

Heat a large nonstick frying pan over a medium heat. Using a scrunched up piece of kitchen paper, dip into the oil and use to wipe over the pan. Drop 3 large tablespoons of the batter into the pan to make 3 pancakes, spreading the batter out slightly with a spoon. Cook for 2–3 minutes until bubbles start to appear on the surface and the underside is golden brown, then flip over and cook for a further 2 minutes. Remove from the pan and keep warm. Repeat with the remaining batter to make 8 pancakes.

Serve the pancakes topped with extra sliced banana, sprinkled with pecans and drizzled with a little honey.

For instant banana pancakes, warm 8 no added sugar ready-made pancakes according to the packet instructions. Slice 4 bananas and divide between the pancakes. Fold them over and serve 2 pancakes per person drizzled with 1 teaspoon clear honey and 40 g (1 ½ oz) fat-free Greek yogurt. **Calories per serving 326**

recipes
under 500
calories

celery, apple & blue cheese salad

Calories per serving **488**
Serves **4**
Preparation time **10 minutes**
Cooking time **3–4 minutes**

60 g (2¼ oz) **walnut halves**
300 g (10 oz) **blue cheese**
3 tablespoons **white wine vinegar**
3 tablespoons **olive oil**
1 tablespoon **walnut oil**
½ teaspoon **clear honey**
4 **celery sticks**, thickly sliced diagonally
2 **green dessert apples**, cored and cut into wedges
40 g (1½ oz) **watercress**
40 g (1½ oz) **rocket leaves**
pepper

Heat a nonstick frying pan over a medium-low heat and dry-fry the walnuts for 3–4 minutes, stirring frequently, until golden and toasted. Set aside.

Place 100 g (3½ oz) of the blue cheese, the vinegar, oils, honey and pepper in a food processor or blender and whizz to a smooth creamy dressing, adding a little water if too thick.

Mix together the celery, apples, watercress and rocket in a large bowl. Toss with the dressing and crumble over the remaining cheese.

Sprinkle over the toasted walnuts and serve.

For celery & Stilton soup, melt 40 g (1½ oz) butter in a saucepan, add 4 chopped celery sticks and sauté for 5 minutes until softened. Stir in 1 peeled and chopped potato, 300 ml (½ pint) milk and 600 ml (1 pint) vegetable stock and bring to the boil, then reduce the heat and simmer for 15–18 minutes until the vegetables are tender. Using a hand-held blender, blend until smooth. Crumble in 225 g (7½ oz) Stilton cheese and season to taste. Ladle into 4 bowls and serve. **Calories per serving 394**

salmon, puy lentil & dill salad

Calories per serving **460**
Serves **4**
Preparation time **30 minutes,**
   plus cooling and chilling
Cooking time **30–40 minutes**

500 g (1 lb) **salmon fillet**
2 tablespoons **dry white wine**
4 **red peppers**
175 g (6 oz) **Puy lentils**
large handful of **dill,** chopped
1 bunch of **spring onions,**
   finely sliced
lemon juice
pepper

Dressing
2 **green chillies**, deseeded
   and chopped
large handful of **flat leaf**
   parsley, chopped
large handful of **dill,** chopped
2 **garlic cloves**
1 teaspoon **Dijon mustard**
8 tablespoons **lemon juice**
1 tablespoon **olive oil**

Place the salmon on a sheet of foil and spoon over the wine. Gather up the foil and fold over at the top to seal. Place on a baking sheet and bake in a preheated oven, 200°C (400°F), Gas Mark 6, for 15–20 minutes until cooked through. Leave to cool, then flake, cover and chill.

Grill the peppers and peel away the skins following the instructions on page 202. Reserve the pepper juices.

Meanwhile, put the lentils in a large saucepan with plenty of water, bring to the boil, then simmer gently for 15–20 minutes until cooked but still firm to the bite.

Make the dressing. Whizz the chillies, parsley, dill, garlic, mustard and lemon juice in a food processor until smooth. With the motor still running, drizzle in the oil through the feeder tube until the mixture is thick.

Drain the lentils, transfer to a bowl and add the peppers and their juices. Add the dill, most of the spring onions and season with pepper. Stir in the dressing and leave to infuse.

Mix the flaked salmon through the lentils, adding a little lemon juice and the remaining spring onions.

For salmon & potato salad, boil 400 g (13 oz) new potatoes for 15–20 minutes until tender. Drain and cool slightly, then lightly crush. Mix in 4 tablespoons olive oil, 2 tablespoons small capers, 1 bunch of sliced spring onions and salt and pepper. Prepare the salmon as above and flake it through the potatoes. Add a handful of chopped dill and 100 g (3½ oz) watercress, then serve. **Calories per serving 383**

tomato & mozzarella salad

Calories per serving **429**
Serves **4**
Preparation time **10 minutes**
Cooking time **2 minutes**

2 tablespoons **pine nuts**
8 ripe **plum tomatoes**, sliced
6 **cherry tomatoes**, halved
1 small **red onion**, thinly sliced
small bunch of **basil**, leaves
 only
40 g (1½ oz) **rocket leaves**
2 x 250 g (8 oz) **mozzarella
 cheese balls**, torn
2 tablespoons **extra virgin
 olive oil**
2 tablespoons **balsamic
 vinegar**
salt and **pepper**

Heat a nonstick frying pan over a medium-low heat and dry-fry the pine nuts, stirring frequently, until lightly golden and toasted. Set aside.

Place the tomatoes, onion and basil in a serving bowl, season with salt and pepper and toss together.

Add the rocket and mozzarella and gently toss again.

Sprinkle over the pine nuts, drizzle with the olive oil and vinegar and serve.

For tomato & basil soup, heat 1 tablespoon olive oil in a saucepan, add 1 diced red onion and 2 chopped garlic cloves and fry for 2–3 minutes until softened. Add 2 x 400 g (13 oz) cans chopped tomatoes, 2 tablespoons tomato purée and 500 ml (17 fl oz) vegetable stock and bring to the boil, then reduce the heat and simmer for 30 minutes. Remove from the heat and stir in a handful of basil leaves and ½ teaspoon honey. Using a hand-held blender, blend until smooth. Season to taste and stir through 60 g (2¼ oz) chopped mozzarella cheese. Ladle into 4 bowls and serve.
Calories per serving 141

curried egg salad

Calories per serving **473**
Serves **4**
Preparation time **10 minutes,
  plus cooling**
Cooking time **7–8 minutes**

8 eggs
4 **tomatoes**, cut into wedges
2 **Little Gem lettuces**, leaves
  separated
¼ **cucumber**, sliced
200 ml (7 fl oz) **natural yogurt**
1 tablespoon **mild curry
  powder**
3 tablespoons **tomato purée**
juice of 2 **limes**
6 tablespoons **no added
  sugar mayonnaise**
thyme leaves, to garnish
salt and **pepper**

Bring a saucepan of water to a simmer, then gently lower the unshelled eggs into the water and cook for 7–8 minutes until hard-boiled. Drain and cool quickly under cold running water.

Shell the eggs, then halve and place on a large serving plate with the tomatoes, lettuce leaves and cucumber.

Mix together the yogurt, curry powder, tomato purée, lime juice and mayonnaise. Season the dressing, then pour it over the salad. Serve immediately, garnished with thyme leaves.

For Indian-style spicy open omelette, heat 2 tablespoons vegetable oil in a large ovenproof frying pan, add 1 chopped onion, 1 chopped red chilli, 2 teaspoons cumin seeds, 1 teaspoon each of peeled and grated fresh root ginger and garlic, 1 teaspoon curry powder and 1 finely chopped tomato. Stir-fry for 3–4 minutes. Beat together 6 eggs and a small handful of finely chopped coriander. Season, then pour over the vegetable mixture and cook over a low heat for 8–10 minutes, or until the base is starting to set. Place under a preheated hot grill for 3–4 minutes, or until the top is set and lightly coloured. Serve with warm naan bread and a salad, if liked. **Calories per serving 197 (not including naan and salad)**

grilled goats' cheese salad

Calories per serving **453**
Serves **4**
Preparation time **15 minutes**
Cooking time **4–5 minutes**

50 g (2 oz) **pine nuts**
2 teaspoons **orange blossom honey**
juice of 1 **lemon**
3 tablespoons **olive oil**
1 teaspoon **no added sugar wholegrain mustard**
1 **cucumber**, halved lengthways, deseeded and thinly sliced
200 g (7 oz) **radishes**, trimmed and thinly sliced
1 **red onion**, thinly sliced
2 tablespoons chopped **mint**
4 round **fromage de chèvre**, about 75 g (3 oz) each

Heat a nonstick frying pan over a medium-low heat and dry-fry the pine nuts, stirring frequently, until lightly golden and toasted. Set aside.

Whisk together the honey, lemon juice, olive oil and mustard in a small bowl. Set aside.

Place the cucumber in a large bowl and add the radish slices, onion, toasted pine nuts and chopped mint and mix well.

Put the fromage de chèvre rounds on a baking sheet and cook under a preheated hot grill for 3–4 minutes until golden and bubbling.

Pour the dressing over the salad and toss well. Divide between 4 plates and top each with a fromage de chèvre.

For goats' cheese stuffed mushrooms, heat 1 tablespoon olive oil in a frying pan, add 4 portobello mushrooms and fry for 3–4 minutes on each side. Divide 200 g (7 oz) goats' cheese evenly between the mushrooms and sprinkle over the leaves of 1 thyme sprig, 2 teaspoons clear honey, ¼ teaspoon freshly ground pepper, 1 crushed garlic clove and 50 g (2 oz) chopped walnuts. Cook under a preheated grill for 3–4 minutes, or until the cheese is melted and bubbling. **Calories per serving 295**

smoked trout & grape salad

Calories per serving **443**
Serves **2**
Preparation time **15 minutes**

200 g (7 oz) **smoked trout**
160 g (5½ oz) **red seedless grapes**
75 g (3 oz) **watercress**
1 **fennel bulb**
3 tablespoons **no added sugar mayonnaise**
4 **cornichons**, finely diced
1½ tablespoons **capers**, chopped
2 tablespoons **lemon juice**
salt and **pepper**

Flake the smoked trout into bite-sized pieces, removing any bones, and place in a large salad bowl.

Wash and drain the grapes and watercress and add them to the bowl. Finely slice the fennel and add to the mix.

Mix together the mayonnaise, cornichons, capers and lemon juice in a small bowl. Season to taste with salt and pepper, then carefully mix through the salad and serve.

For crispy trout salad, add 1 finely chopped hard-boiled egg, 2 finely chopped anchovy fillets and 1 tablespoon chopped parsley to the dressing. Prepare the salad as above, adding 1 green dessert apple, cut into matchsticks. Season 2 x 140 g (5 oz) pieces of fresh trout with salt and pepper. Heat 1 tablespoon vegetable oil in a frying pan over a high heat and cook the trout, skin side down, for 4 minutes, pressing it down with a fish slice to give an evenly crispy skin. Turn over the fish and cook for a further 2 minutes, or until it is just cooked through. Remove from the pan. Toss the salad with the dressing and serve immediately with the crispy trout. **Calories per serving 432**

chicken & spinach chowder

Calories per serving **427**
Serves **6**
Preparation time **15 minutes**
Cooking time **35 minutes**

1 tablespoon **sunflower oil**
25 g (1 oz) **butter**
4 **smoked back bacon rashers**, chopped
2 small **leeks**, trimmed, cleaned and thinly sliced, green and white parts separated
750 g (1½ lb) **potatoes**, peeled and diced
900 ml (1½ pints) **chicken stock**
200 g (7 oz) **ready-cooked chicken**, diced
600 ml (1 pint) **semi-skimmed milk**
150 ml (¼ pint) **double cream**
100 g (3½ oz) **spinach**, roughly chopped
grated **nutmeg**
salt and **pepper**

Heat the oil and butter in a large saucepan, add the bacon, white leeks and diced potatoes and cook over a low heat for 5 minutes, stirring until lightly golden.

Mix in the stock, then bring to the boil, cover and simmer for 20 minutes until the potatoes are just tender. Add the chicken and boil rapidly for 3 minutes.

Stir in the green leeks, milk, cream and a little salt and pepper. Simmer gently for 5 minutes, then stir in the spinach and a little nutmeg. Cook for 2 minutes until the spinach is just cooked.

Ladle into 6 bowls, sprinkle with a little extra nutmeg and serve.

For creamy chicken, bacon & celeriac soup, use 1 chopped onion in place of the leeks and replace the potatoes with celeriac. Fry with the bacon as above. Roughly mash or purée the soup, then add the chicken and cook as above. Mix with cream and nutmeg but omit the spinach, adding 2 tablespoons chopped chives instead. **Calories per serving 353**

chicken parmigiana

Calories per serving **499**
Serves **4**
Preparation time **15 minutes,
plus chilling**
Cooking time **13–14 minutes**

4 **boneless, skinless chicken
breasts**, about 150 g (5 oz)
each
2 **eggs**
75 g (3 oz) **brown
breadcrumbs**
75 g (3 oz) **Parmesan
cheese**, grated
1 tablespoon **olive oil**
2 **garlic cloves**, crushed
600 ml (1 pint) **passata**
1 teaspoon **dried oregano**
100 g (3½ oz) **mozzarella
cheese**, grated
crisp green salad, to serve

Place the chicken breasts between 2 sheets of clingfilm or greaseproof paper and bash with a rolling pin or mallet until they are about 4–5 mm (¼ inch) thick.

Beat the eggs in a shallow bowl, then mix together the breadcrumbs and half the grated Parmesan and place in a separate shallow bowl. Dip the chicken breasts first in the egg and then in the breadcrumb and Parmesan mixture. Cover and chill for 15 minutes.

Cook the chicken under a preheated hot grill for 5 minutes on each side until cooked through.

Meanwhile, heat the oil in a pan, add the garlic and fry for 1 minute, then add the passata and oregano and simmer for 5 minutes.

Pour the tomato sauce into an ovenproof dish and top with the chicken. Sprinkle over the mozzarella and remaining Parmesan and grill for 3–4 minutes until the cheese has melted and the sauce is bubbling. Serve with a crisp green salad.

For chicken & Parmesan pasta, cook 300 g (10 oz) gluten-free pasta in a saucepan of boiling water according to the packet instructions, adding 300 g (10 oz) broccoli florets 3 minutes before the end of the cooking time. Meanwhile, heat 1 tablespoon olive oil in a frying pan and cook 400 g (13 oz) chopped chicken breast for 8–10 minutes until golden and cooked through, adding 2 crushed garlic cloves 2 minutes before the end of the cooking time. Drain the pasta and broccoli and tip into the chicken, then stir in 2 tablespoons flaked almonds, 2 tablespoons chopped sun-dried tomatoes and 2 tablespoons grated Parmesan. **Calories per serving 498**

cod rarebit

Calories per serving **499**
Serves **4**
Preparation time **5 minutes**
Cooking time **15 minutes**

2 tablespoons **no added
    sugar wholegrain mustard**
3 tablespoons **beer** or **semi-
    skimmed milk**
250 g (8 oz) **Cheddar
    cheese**, grated
2 tablespoons **olive oil**
4 pieces of **cod fillet**, about
    200 g (7 oz) each, pin-boned
salt and **pepper**

Mix together the mustard, beer or milk and cheese
in a small saucepan. Over a low heat, leave the cheese
to melt. Stir occasionally and don't let it boil, as the
cheese will curdle. Remove the pan from the heat and
leave to cool and thicken.

Heat a frying pan over a high heat with the oil. Season
the fish and place it in the pan, skin side down, and
cook for 4–5 minutes until the skin is crispy, then turn
the fish over and cook for a further 1 minute until
cooked through.

Spread the cheese mixture over the 4 pieces of
cod and place under a preheated grill and cook until
golden brown.

For wholegrain mustard & cream sauce, to serve
as an accompaniment, in a small saucepan sweat
2 finely chopped shallots and 1 crushed garlic clove in
1 tablespoon olive oil. Add 100 ml (3½ fl oz) chicken
stock and 200 ml (7 fl oz) double cream to the pan and
bring to the boil. Stir in 1 tablespoon no added sugar
wholegrain mustard. **Calories per serving 262**

peppered beef with potato cakes

Calories per serving **455**
Serves **4**
Preparation time **15 minutes**
Cooking time **15–20 minutes**

8 tablespoons **balsamic vinegar**
2 tablespoons **cracked black pepper**
2 lean **rump steaks**, about 200 g (7 oz) each
550 g (1 lb 2 oz) **sweet potatoes**, peeled and coarsely grated
2 **eggs**, beaten
2 tablespoons **gram flour**
40 g (1½ oz) **Parmesan cheese**, grated
2 tablespoons **groundnut oil**
100 g (3½ oz) **rocket leaves**
salt and **pepper**

Pour the balsamic into a small pan and bubble until reduced by half and it forms a syrupy glaze. Set aside.

Place the cracked pepper on a board or plate and press each steak into it. Heat a griddle pan and cook the steaks for 3–4 minutes on each side depending on how rare you like your steak. Leave to rest for 5 minutes, then slice into thick slices.

Meanwhile, mix together the sweet potatoes, eggs, gram flour, Parmesan and salt and pepper in a bowl. Heat the oil in a large frying pan, add spoonfuls of the mixture to the pan and flatten with a spatula. Cook for 2–3 minutes on each side until crisp and golden. Remove from the pan and keep warm. Repeat with the remaining mixture.

Arrange 2 sweet potato cakes on each plate, then top with the rocket and slices of steak. Serve drizzled with the balsamic glaze.

For stuffed sweet potatoes, bake 4 sweet potatoes in a preheated oven, 200°C (400°F), Gas Mark 6, for 1 hour until soft. When cool enough to handle, cut in half lengthways and scoop out the flesh into a bowl. Reserve the skins. Add 4 chopped spring onions, 100 g (3½ oz) grated Manchego cheese and 2 tablespoons soured cream to the bowl and mix together, then spoon back into the potato skins. Cook 6 pancetta rashers under a preheated hot grill until crisp. Sprinkle on top of the potatoes to serve. **Calories per serving 320**

potato pizza margherita

Calories per serving **478**
Serves **4**
Preparation time **20 minutes,
plus cooling**
Cooking time **45 minutes**

1 kg (2 lb) **baking potatoes**,
peeled and cut into small
chunks
3 tablespoons **olive oil**, plus
extra for oiling
1 **egg**, beaten
50 g (2 oz) **Parmesan** or
Cheddar cheese, grated
4 tablespoons **no added
sugar tomato ketchup**
500 g (1 lb) small **tomatoes**,
thinly sliced
125 g (4 oz) **mozzarella
cheese**, thinly sliced
1 tablespoon chopped **thyme**,
plus extra sprigs to garnish
(optional)
salt

Cook the potatoes in a saucepan of salted boiling
water for 15 minutes, or until tender. Drain well, return
to the pan and leave to cool for 10 minutes.

Add 2 tablespoons of the oil, the egg and half the
grated cheese to the potato and mix well. Turn out
on to an oiled baking sheet and spread out to form
a 25 cm (10 inch) round. Place in a preheated oven,
200°C (400°F), Gas Mark 6, for 15 minutes.

Remove from the oven and spread with the ketchup.
Arrange the tomatoes and mozzarella slices on top.
Scatter with the remaining grated cheese, thyme, if
using, and a little salt. Drizzle with the remaining oil.

Return to the oven for a further 15 minutes until the
potato is crisp around the edges and the cheese is
melting. Cut into 4 wedges, garnish with thyme sprigs,
if liked, and serve.

For salami potato pizza, make as above, adding
4 slices of chopped salami with the tomato and
mozzarella to the top of the pizza. Continue as above.
Calories per serving 499

moroccan chicken & harissa

Calories per serving **433 (not including rice)**
Serves **4**
Preparation time **20 minutes, plus cooling**
Cooking time **40 minutes**

1 **onion**, very finely chopped
2 teaspoons **paprika**
1 teaspoon **cumin seeds**
4 **boneless, skinless chicken breasts**, about 125 g (4 oz) each
bunch of **coriander**, finely chopped
4 tablespoons **lemon juice**
3 tablespoons **olive oil**
salt and **pepper**

Harissa
4 **red peppers**
4 large **red chillies**
2 **garlic cloves**, crushed
½ teaspoon **coriander seeds**
1 teaspoon **caraway seeds**
5 tablespoons **olive oil**

Make the harissa. Heat a griddle pan or frying pan, add the whole red peppers and cook for 15 minutes, turning occasionally. The skins will blacken and start to lift. Place the peppers in a plastic bag, seal the bag and set aside for a while (this encourages them to 'sweat', making it easier to remove their skins). When cool enough to handle, remove the skin, cores and seeds from the peppers and place the flesh in a blender or food processor.

Remove the skin, cores and seeds from the red chillies in the same way and add the chilli flesh to the blender, together with the garlic, coriander and caraway seeds and olive oil. Process in the blender to a smooth paste. If not required immediately, place the harissa in a sealable container and pour a thin layer of olive oil over the top. Cover with a lid and refrigerate.

Place the onion in a bowl, add the paprika and cumin seeds and mix together. Rub the onion and spice mixture into the chicken breasts. Heat the cleaned pan, add the chicken and cook for 10 minutes on each side, turning once, until cooked through.

Put the coriander in a bowl and add the lemon juice, olive oil and a little seasoning. Add the chicken to the bowl and toss well. Serve with the harissa and brown rice, if liked.

For a spinach salad, to serve as an accompaniment, rinse and tear 400 g (13 oz) spinach and add to a pan with any residual water. Cover and cook for 1–2 minutes until wilted. Stir in 1 chopped garlic clove, 100 g (3½ oz) Greek yogurt, season and warm through. **Calories per serving 55**

spicy sprouting broccoli pasta

Calories per serving **405**
Serves **4**
Preparation time **5 minutes**
Cooking time **10–12 minutes**

350 g (11½ oz) **spaghetti**
200 g (7 oz) **purple sprouting broccoli**
2 tablespoons **olive oil**
8 **spring onions**, chopped
½ teaspoon **dried chilli flakes**
juice of ½ **lemon**
salt and **pepper**
25 g (1 oz) **Parmesan cheese**, grated, to serve

Cook the spaghetti in a saucepan of boiling water according to the packet instructions.

Meanwhile, blanch the broccoli in a separate pan of boiling water for 2 minutes, then drain and refresh under cold running water.

Heat the oil in a frying pan, add the sprouting broccoli and spring onions and cook over a medium heat for 4–5 minutes until softened.

Drain the pasta, then stir into the vegetables with the chilli flakes and lemon juice. Season well and serve sprinkled with the grated Parmesan.

For broccoli & pasta salad, cook 350 g (11½ oz) pasta shapes in a saucepan of boiling water according to the packet instructions, adding 200 g (7 oz) trimmed Tenderstem broccoli 2 minutes before the end of the cooking time. Drain and refresh under cold running water, then toss together with 100 g (3½ oz) crumbled feta cheese, 4 sliced spring onions, 10 halved pitted olives, 2 tablespoons olive oil and 1 tablespoon balsamic vinegar. Serve sprinkled with 2 tablespoons toasted pecan nuts. **Calories per serving 495**

lime & coriander sea bass

Calories per serving **486**
Serves **4**
Preparation time **20 minutes,
  plus chilling**
Cooking time **10 minutes**

150 g (5 oz) butter, softened
3 tablespoons chopped
  coriander, plus small bunch
1 large **red chilli**, deseeded
  and finely chopped
2 **limes**
4 whole **sea bass**, about
  300 g (10 oz) each, gutted
  and scaled
2 tablespoons **vegetable oil**
salt and **pepper**

Mix together the butter, chopped coriander, chilli and grated rind of the limes in a bowl. Season with salt and pepper. Take a sheet of clingfilm and spoon on the butter mixture. Roll the clingfilm up to form a sausage, then twist the ends to enclose the butter and place in the refrigerator to set.

Make 3 slits in the flesh on each side of the fish, making sure you don't cut all the way through it. Slice the grated limes and place a few slices of lime in the cavity of each fish, along with some coriander sprigs.

Brush the outside of the fish lightly with the oil and season both sides generously with salt and pepper. Place the fish directly on the rack of a medium-hot barbecue or in a fish grill first (this is easier). Cook the fish for 5 minutes on each side. The best way to test if the fish is cooked is by looking inside the cavity to see if the flesh has become opaque or if the fish is firm to the touch.

Slice the butter thinly into rounds and place a slice in each of the cuts you made on 1 side of the fish. Allow the butter to melt. Serve with a green salad.

For barbecued sea bass parcels, butter 4 large square pieces of foil and place a sea bass in the centre of each piece. Drizzle over 2 tablespoons olive oil and place a few pieces of chopped chilli and ginger and a couple of slices of lime in each parcel. Seal the foil to form parcels and place on a medium-hot barbecue for 8–10 minutes, or until the fish turns opaque. **Calories per serving 206**

corned beef hash

Calories per serving **481**
Serves **4**
Preparation time **10 minutes**
Cooking time **20–25 minutes**

625 g (1 ¼ lb) **potatoes**,
  peeled
3 tablespoons **olive oil**
1 **onion**, chopped
340 g (11 ½ oz) can **corned
beef**
2 **tomatoes**, chopped
4 **eggs**

Cook the potatoes in a saucepan of boiling water for 12–14 minutes until tender.

Meanwhile, heat 1 tablespoon of oil in a large frying pan, add the onion and cook for 4–5 minutes until softened. Add the corned beef to the pan and cook for a further 2–3 minutes.

Drain the potatoes and add them to the pan, cooking and lightly crushing them for 1–2 minutes. Stir in the tomatoes and cook for a further 3–4 minutes.

Meanwhile, heat the remaining oil in another frying pan and fry the eggs to your liking.

Serve the corned beef hash topped with a fried egg.

For corned beef, egg & salad baguettes, slice 2 gluten-free baguettes in half horizontally and toast each piece for 2–3 minutes on each side. Spread the bottom half of each baguette with a teaspoon of butter, then top with ¼ shredded iceberg lettuce, 1 sliced hard-boiled egg and one-quarter of a 340 g (11 ½ oz) can corned beef, sliced. Sandwich together with the remaining baguettes and cut each baguette in half.
Calories per half baguette 487

salmon with broad bean salad

Calories per serving **461**
Serves **4**
Preparation time **15 minutes**
Cooking time **10–15 minutes**

650 g (1¼ lb) podded **fresh**
   or **frozen broad beans**
2 tablespoons chopped **mint**
1 tablespoon chopped **dill**
3 tablespoons **lemon juice**
3 tablespoons **olive oil**
2 teaspoons **Dijon mustard**
4 **salmon fillets**, about 150 g
   (5 oz) each, skin on
1 teaspoon **sea salt**
1 teaspoon **cracked black**
   pepper
lemon wedges, to serve

Cook the broad beans in a saucepan of boiling water for 5–6 minutes, or until tender, then drain and remove the skins. Place the beans in a bowl and toss with the mint, dill, lemon juice, 2 tablespoons of the oil and the mustard.

Sprinkle the skin of the salmon with the salt and pepper. Heat the remaining oil in a large frying pan, add the salmon, skin side down, and cook for 4–5 minutes until the skin is golden and crisp. Turn the fish over and cook for a further 2–3 minutes, or until the salmon is cooked through and to your liking.

Divide the broad bean salad between 4 plates, top with the salmon and serve with lemon wedges.

For salmon & broad bean fishcakes, cook 400 g (13 oz) peeled and chopped potatoes in a saucepan of boiling water for 15–18 minutes until tender, adding 225 g (7½ oz) broad beans 5 minutes before the end of the cooking time. Drain and mash together. Meanwhile, cook 300 g (10 oz) skinless salmon fillet under a preheated hot grill for 4–5 minutes on each side, or until cooked through, then flake into big pieces and stir into the mash with 1 tablespoon chopped dill and salt and pepper. Shape into 4 fishcakes and dust with 1 tablespoon gram flour. Heat 2 tablespoons olive oil in a frying pan and cook the fishcakes for 3–4 minutes on each side until heated through. Serve with a crisp green salad. **Calories per serving 377**

roasted summer vegetables

Calories per serving **418**
Serves **4**
Preparation time **15 minutes**
Cooking time **45–50 minutes**

1 **red pepper**, cored,
   deseeded and thickly sliced
1 **yellow pepper**, cored,
   deseeded and thickly sliced
1 **aubergine**, cut into chunks
2 **yellow** or **green courgettes**,
   cut into chunks
1 **red onion**, cut into wedges
6 **garlic cloves**
2 tablespoons **extra virgin**
   rapeseed or **olive oil**
4–5 **thyme sprigs**
150 g (5 oz) **yellow** and **red**
   baby plum tomatoes
150 g (5 oz) **hazelnuts**
125 g (4 oz) **rocket leaves**
2 tablespoons **raspberry** or
   balsamic vinegar
salt and **pepper**
handful of **mustard cress**, to
   garnish (optional)

Toss all the vegetables, except the tomatoes, in a large bowl with the oil. Season with a little salt and pepper and add the thyme. Tip into a large roasting tin and place in a preheated oven, 190°C (375°F), Gas Mark 5, for 40–45 minutes, or until the vegetables are tender. Add the tomatoes and return to the oven for a further 5 minutes, or until the tomatoes are just softened and beginning to burst.

Meanwhile, tip the hazelnuts into a small roasting tin and place in the oven for about 10–12 minutes, or until golden and the skin is peeling away. Leave to cool, then remove the excess skin and crush lightly.

Toss the rocket leaves gently with the roasted vegetables and heap on to 4 large plates. Scatter over the crushed hazelnuts and drizzle with the vinegar. Scatter over the mustard cress, if liked, and serve immediately.

For roasted vegetable pasta, roast the vegetables as above, then tip into a large saucepan with 500 ml (17 fl oz) passata and 150 ml (¼ pint) vegetable stock. Bring to the boil, then reduce the heat and simmer gently for 20 minutes. Remove from the heat and, using a hand-held blender, blend until smooth. Season with salt and pepper to taste and serve with 700 g (1½ lb) hot cooked pasta. **Calories per serving 461**

lamb with pea & rosemary mash

Calories per serving **491**
Serves **4**
Preparation time **10 minutes**
Cooking time **12–15 minutes**

750 g (1 lb 10 oz) **potatoes**,
  peeled and chopped
350 g (11½ oz) **frozen** or
  fresh peas
1 tablespoon chopped
  rosemary
8 **lamb cutlets**, about 100 g
  (3½ oz) each
30 g (1 oz) **butter**
salt and **pepper**

Cook the potatoes in a saucepan of boiling water for 12–15 minutes until tender, adding the peas 2 minutes before the end of the cooking time.

Meanwhile, sprinkle half the rosemary over the lamb cutlets, then cook them under a preheated hot grill for 3–4 minutes on each side depending on how pink you like your lamb. Leave to rest.

Drain the potatoes and peas, then return to the pan and lightly mash with the remaining rosemary, butter and salt and pepper to taste. Serve the lamb cutlets with the pea and rosemary mash.

For rosemary lamb cutlets with summer salad, mix together 2 tablespoons chopped rosemary and 1 tablespoon olive oil in a small bowl, then rub over 8 lamb cutlets. Cook under a preheated hot grill for 3–4 minutes on each side depending on how pink you like your lamb. Meanwhile, cook 100 g (3½ oz) fresh or frozen peas, 75 g (3 oz) broad beans and 125 g (4 oz) asparagus tips in a saucepan of boiling water for 2–3 minutes. Drain, refresh under cold running water and drain again, then toss together with 2 carrots, peeled and cut into matchsticks, 12 baby sweetcorn, the torn leaves of 1 Romaine lettuce, a small handful of mint leaves and 12 cherry tomatoes in a serving bowl. Drizzle with 2 tablespoons extra virgin olive oil and the juice of 1 lemon. Serve with the lamb. **Calories per serving 376**

turkey croque madame

Calories per serving **499**
Serves **4**
Preparation time **10 minutes**
Cooking time **8–10 minutes**

8 x 40 g (1½ oz) **wholegrain bread slices**, from a large, round loaf

3 tablespoons **no added sugar wholegrain mustard**

200 g (7 oz) **reduced-fat mature Cheddar cheese**, finely grated

200 g (7 oz) **cooked turkey**, thinly sliced

2 **tomatoes**, sliced

2 **spring onions**, thinly sliced

1 tablespoon **distilled vinegar**

4 large **eggs**

100 g (3½ oz) **baby leaf spinach**

pepper

chopped **chives**, to garnish

Lay 4 slices of the bread on a board and spread each slice with the mustard. Top the slices with half of the Cheddar, the turkey and tomato slices, then scatter with the spring onions. Season with pepper and scatter over the remaining Cheddar. Top with the remaining slices of bread.

Heat a large, nonstick frying pan over a medium heat until hot, then carefully add the sandwiches and cook for 4–5 minutes, or until golden and crispy. Turn the sandwiches over and cook for a further 4–5 minutes. Alternatively, toast in a flat-surfaced panini machine according to the manufacturer's instructions.

Meanwhile, bring a large saucepan of water to a gentle simmer, add the vinegar and stir with a large spoon to create a swirl. Carefully break 2 eggs into the water and cook for 3 minutes. Remove with a slotted spoon and keep warm. Repeat with the remaining eggs.

Transfer each sandwich to a serving plate, scatter over a few spinach leaves and top with a poached egg. Garnish with chives and serve immediately.

For turkey & cheese sandwiches, cut 1 wholegrain baguette almost in half lengthways. Cut into 4 and place, opened out, on a baking sheet. Top as above with the mustard, turkey, tomatoes and spring onions. Scatter with all of the grated cheese. Cook under a preheated hot grill for 3–4 minutes or until hot and melted. Serve hot with baby leaf spinach, if liked.
Calories per serving 437

hake on creamed spinach

Calories per serving **499**
Serves **4**
Preparation time **4 minutes**
Cooking time **15 minutes**

4 pieces of **hake**, about 200 g
 (7 oz) each
2 tablespoons **olive oil**
2 **shallots**, finely chopped
1 **garlic clove**, crushed
50 ml (2 fl oz) **white wine**
500 g (1 lb) **baby spinach
 leaves**
100 ml (3½ fl oz) **double
 cream**
75 g (3 oz) **pine nuts**
salt and **pepper**

Place the hake in an ovenproof dish, drizzle with
1 tablespoon of the oil and season with salt and pepper.
Place in a preheated oven, 200°C (400°F), Gas Mark 6,
for 6–8 minutes, or until the fish is firm.

Meanwhile, heat the remaining oil in a large frying pan,
add the shallots and fry gently until softened. Add the
garlic and fry for a further 1 minute. Pour in the wine
and leave to bubble until all the liquid has evaporated.

Add the spinach to the pan in batches, allowing it to wilt
completely, then stir in the cream and season with salt
and pepper.

Heat a nonstick frying pan over a medium-low heat
and dry-fry the pine nuts, stirring frequently, until lightly
golden and toasted.

Place some creamed spinach in the centre of each
plate, top with a piece of fish and scatter some toasted
pine nuts over the top.

beetroot risotto

Calories per serving **498**
Serves **4**
Preparation time **15 minutes**
Cooking time **1 hour**

500 g (1 lb) **raw beetroot**,
  peeled and diced
2 tablespoons **olive oil**
2 tablespoons **water**
pinch of **dried sage**
1 large **onion**, diced
2 **garlic cloves**, crushed
300 g (10 oz) **risotto rice**
1 litre (1¾ pints) hot
  vegetable stock
100 g (3½ oz) **goats' cheese**
salt and **pepper**

To serve
20g (¾ oz) **Parmesan**
  cheese, grated
2–3 chopped **sage leaves**

Toss the beetroot in half the oil and season well. Wrap in foil and cook in a preheated oven, 200°C (400°F), Gas Mark 6, for 30–35 minutes until tender.

Place half of the beetroot in a food processor or blender with the measurement water and dried sage and blend to a purée. Set aside.

Heat the remaining oil in a saucepan, add the onion and fry for 3–4 minutes until softened. Add the garlic and rice and stir well. Add a ladle of the stock and cook, stirring, until all the liquid has been absorbed. Continue to add the remaining stock in the same way until the rice is almost tender.

Stir in the cooked diced beetroot and the beetroot purée and continue to cook, stirring, for 8–10 minutes until the rice is cooked through. Stir in the goats' cheese and serve sprinkled with the Parmesan cheese and chopped sage.

For roasted beetroot & goats' cheese salad, put 300 g (10 oz) raw beetroot, peeled and cut into wedges, in a roasting tin and toss with 1 tablespoon olive oil and 1 teaspoon cumin seeds. Roast as above for 35–40 minutes. Meanwhile, whisk together 2 tablespoons olive oil, 1 tablespoon balsamic vinegar, ½ teaspoon no added sugar wholegrain mustard and ½ teaspoon maple syrup in a small bowl. Segment 2 oranges and toss with 60 g (2¼ oz) watercress, 1 peeled, stoned and sliced avocado, 2 tablespoons pumpkin seeds and ¼ sliced cucumber in a serving bowl. Grill 4 x 60 g (2¼ oz) goats' cheese rounds until golden. Add the roasted beetroot to the salad and toss with the dressing. Top with the goats' cheese and serve. **Calories per serving 468**

indian fish curry

Calories per serving **446** (not **including rice**)

Serves **4**

Preparation time **15 minutes**

Cooking time **30 minutes**

2 tablespoons **vegetable oil**
1 **onion**, finely chopped
1 **red chilli**, deseeded and finely chopped
1 **garlic clove**, crushed
5 cm (2 inch) piece of **fresh root ginger**, peeled and finely chopped
1 tablespoon **ground cumin**
1 tablespoon **ground coriander**
1 teaspoon **turmeric**
1 teaspoon **garam masala**
400 g (13 oz) can **chopped tomatoes**
400 ml (14 fl oz) can **coconut milk**
2 large **monkfish tails**, cut into chunks
12 **raw peeled king prawns**
250 g (8 oz) **live mussels**, scrubbed and debearded (discard any that don't shut when tapped)
small bunch of **coriander** or **parsley**, roughly chopped

Heat the oil in a large frying pan, add the onion and fry gently for about 10 minutes until golden brown. Add the chilli, garlic, ginger and dried spices and fry for a further 1 minute until fragrant.

Add the tomatoes and coconut milk and bring to the boil, then reduce the heat and simmer for about 10 minutes until the curry sauce has thickened.

Stir in the monkfish and prawns and cook for 3–4 minutes until the fish is just cooked through and the prawns turn pink. Add the mussels and cook for a further 3–4 minutes or until they have opened. Discard any that remain closed.

Season and stir through the chopped herbs. Serve with basmati rice, if liked.

For garlic & black mustard seed naan breads, to serve as an accompaniment, heat 1 tablespoon oil in a small frying pan, add 1 tablespoon black mustard seeds and fry until they start to pop. Mix together 100 g (3½ oz) softened butter with the mustard seeds and 1 crushed garlic clove and spread this mixture over 2 large naan breads. Place the 2 buttered sides together and wrap in foil. Bake in a preheated oven, 180°C (350°F), Gas Mark 4, for 10 minutes until warmed through. Cut into 4 and serve. **Calories per serving 380**

lamb kefta pittas

Calories per serving **431**
Serves **4**
Preparation time **20 minutes**
Cooking time **10–12 minutes**

½ tablespoon **groundnut oil**
4 **wholemeal pitta breads**
lemon wedges, to serve

Lamb keftas
1 small **onion**, chopped
2 **garlic cloves**, crushed
400 g (13 oz) **10% fat minced
 lamb**
50 g (2 oz) **fresh wholemeal
 breadcrumbs**
1 small **egg**, lightly beaten
1 small bunch of **parsley**,
 chopped
1 small bunch of **coriander**,
 chopped
¼ tablespoon **ground
 cinnamon**
1 tablespoon **ground paprika**
½ tablespoon **ground cumin**
salt and **pepper**

Salad
1 **carrot**, peeled and grated
6 **radishes**, thinly sliced
½ **iceberg lettuce**, shredded
½ **cucumber**, thinly sliced

Place all the kefta ingredients in a food processor
and pulse several times until well combined. Tip into
a large bowl and, using wet hands, shape the mixture
into 16 meatballs.

Heat the groundnut oil in a large, nonstick frying pan
over a medium heat, add the meatballs and fry for
10–12 minutes, turning frequently, until cooked through
and browned all over. Remove with a slotted spoon and
drain on kitchen paper.

Meanwhile, wrap the pitta breads in foil and place
in a preheated oven, 180°C (350°F), Gas Mark 4, for
5–8 minutes, or until warm. To make the salad, mix the
carrot, radishes, lettuce and cucumber in a bowl.

Split open the warmed pittas, fill with the salad and
then add the meatballs. Serve immediately with lemon
wedges to squeeze over.

For barbecued lamb skewers, make the kefta
mixture as above. Tip into a large bowl and form into
flat sausage shapes around 4 long, flat metal skewers.
Cook on a barbecue for 10–12 minutes, or until cooked
through, then serve with the pitta breads and salad as
above. **Calories per serving 431**

mediterranean cauliflower pizzas

Calories per serving **443**

Serves **4**

Preparation time **20 minutes**

Cooking time **1 hour**

2 heads of **cauliflower**,
  roughly chopped

2 **eggs**

50 g (2 oz) **Cheddar cheese**,
  grated

40 g (1½ oz) **Parmesan
  cheese**, grated

1 teaspoon **cayenne pepper**

large pinch of **sea salt**

4 tablespoons **tomato purée**

1 **red pepper**, cored,
  deseeded and sliced

1 **courgette**, thinly sliced

1 **garlic clove**, finely sliced

4 **artichoke hearts**, quartered

1 teaspoon **dried oregano**

250 g (8 oz) **mozzarella
  cheese**, sliced

Line a large baking sheet with nonstick baking paper.

Place the cauliflower in a food processor or blender and process until very fine. Transfer to a dry frying pan and cook for 10 minutes, stirring occasionally, to get rid of the moisture.

Tip the cauliflower into a large bowl and stir in the eggs, cheeses, cayenne pepper and salt. Divide the mixture in half and spoon on to the prepared baking sheet in 2 mounds, using your hands to shape into rough rounds.

Place in a preheated oven, 180°C (350°F), Gas Mark 4, for 30 minutes until they hold their shape and are golden. Using a palette knife, flip each one over and bake for a further 10 minutes.

Remove from the oven and spread with the tomato purée, then top with the vegetables, oregano and mozzarella. Return to the oven and bake for 10 minutes. Cut each pizza in half, then serve immediately.

For cauliflower cheese soup, heat 1 tablespoon olive oil in a saucepan, add 1 chopped onion and fry for 4–5 minutes until softened. Add 1 large chopped cauliflower, about 875 g (1¾ lb) total weight, 150 g (5 oz) peeled and chopped potatoes and 1.2 litres (2 pints) vegetable stock and bring to the boil. Simmer for 20–25 minutes until the vegetables are soft, then stir in 150 g (5 oz) crumbled feta cheese. Using a hand-held blender, blend until smooth. Season to taste, then serve with a sprinkling of grated Parmesan. **Calories per serving 311**

cheesy pork with parsnip purée

Calories per serving **480 (not including green beans)**
Serves **4**
Preparation time **10 minutes**
Cooking time **16–20 minutes**

4 lean **pork steaks**, about 125 g (4 oz) each
1 teaspoon **olive oil**
50 g (2 oz) **crumbly cheese**, such as Wensleydale or Cheshire, crumbled
½ tablespoon chopped **sage**
75 g (3 oz) **granary breadcrumbs**
1 **egg yolk**, beaten
pepper

Parsnip purée
625 g (1¼ lb) **parsnips**, chopped
2 **garlic cloves**
3 tablespoons **crème fraîche**

Season the pork steaks with plenty of pepper. Heat the oil in a nonstick frying pan, add the pork steaks and fry for 2 minutes on each side until browned, then transfer to an ovenproof dish.

Mix together the cheese, sage, breadcrumbs and egg yolk. Divide the mixture into 4 and use to top each of the pork steaks, pressing down gently. Cook in a preheated oven, 200°C (400°F), Gas Mark 6, for 12–15 minutes until the topping is golden.

Meanwhile, make the purée. Place the parsnips and garlic in a saucepan of boiling water and cook for 10–12 minutes until tender.

Drain and mash with the crème fraîche and plenty of pepper. Serve with the pork steaks and steamed green beans, if liked.

For chicken with breaded tomato topping, replace the pork with 4 x 150 g (5 oz) boneless, skinless chicken breasts. Brown and lay in an ovenproof dish, as above. Make the topping as above, replacing the sage with 4 chopped sun-dried tomatoes and ¼ teaspoon dried oregano. Bake as above and serve with the parsnip purée. **Calories per serving 475**

nutty passion fruit yogurts

Calories per serving **428**
Serves **2**
Preparation time **5 minutes,
  plus chilling**

2 **passion fruit**
250 ml (8 fl oz) **natural yogurt**
4 tablespoons **clear honey**
50 g (2 oz) **roasted
  hazelnuts**, roughly chopped
4 **clementines**, peeled and
  chopped into small pieces

Halve the passion fruit and scoop the pulp into a large bowl. Add the yogurt and mix them together gently.

Put 2 tablespoonfuls of the honey in the bases of 2 narrow glasses and scatter with half of the hazelnuts. Spoon half of the yogurt over the nuts and arrange half of the clementine pieces on top of the yogurt.

Repeat the layering, reserving a few of the nuts for decoration. Scatter the nuts over the top and chill the yogurts until ready to serve.

For passion fruit, coconut & strawberry yogurts, soak 2 tablespoons desiccated coconut in 4 tablespoons skimmed milk for 30 minutes. Mix the passion fruit and yogurt as above, also folding in the soaked coconut. Layer as above, omitting the hazelnuts and replacing the clementines with 100 g (3½ oz) quartered strawberries. **Calories per serving 199**

rosemary panna cottas

Calories per serving **456**
Serves **6**
Preparation time **15 minutes,
plus soaking, cooling and
chilling**
Cooking time **15 minutes**

3 tablespoons **cold water**
1 sachet or 3 teaspoons
  powdered gelatine
450 ml (¾ pint) **double cream**
150 ml (¼ pint) **milk**
4 tablespoons **thick-set
  honey**
2 teaspoons very finely
  chopped **rosemary leaves**
small **rosemary sprigs,** to
  decorate

Apricot compote
200 g (7 oz) r**eady-to-eat
  dried apricots,** sliced
300 ml (½ pint) **water**
1 tablespoon **thick-set honey**
2 teaspoons very finely
  chopped **rosemary leaves**

Spoon the measurement water into a small heatproof bowl or mug. Sprinkle the gelatine over and tilt the bowl or mug so that all the dry powder is absorbed by the water. Leave to soak for 5 minutes.

Pour the cream and milk into a saucepan, add the honey and bring to the boil. Add the soaked gelatine, take the pan off the heat and stir until completely dissolved. Add the rosemary and leave to stand for 20 minutes for the flavours to infuse, stirring from time to time. Pour the cream mixture into 6 individual 150 ml (¼ pint) metal moulds, straining if preferred. Leave to cool completely, then chill for 4–5 hours until set.

Put all the compôte ingredients into a saucepan, cover and simmer for 10 minutes, then leave to cool.

Dip the moulds into hot water for 10 seconds, loosen the edges, then turn out the panna cottas on to small serving plates and spoon the compôte around them. Decorate the panna cottas with the rosemary sprigs.

For vanilla panna cottas, make the panna cotta as above but without the rosemary, adding the seeds from 1 slit vanilla pod and the pod itself as the cream mixture cools. Discard the pod just before pouring the mixture into the moulds, then continue as above. Turn out and serve with fresh raspberries, if liked. **Calories per serving 456 (not including raspberries)**

raw raspberry & nut tarts

Calories per serving **418**
Makes **6**
Preparation time **20 minutes,
 plus soaking and chilling**

175 g (6 oz) **blanched
 almonds**
175 g (6 oz) **cashew nuts**
juice and grated rind of 1 large
 lemon
5 tablespoons **water**
4 teaspoons **maple syrup**
125 g (4 oz) **pitted dates**
150 g (5 oz) **raspberries**
mint leaves, to decorate

Place the almonds in a bowl, pour over enough water to cover and leave to soak for at least 2 hours, or preferably overnight.

Put the cashews, lemon rind and juice, measurement water and 2 teaspoons maple syrup in a food processor or blender and blend together. Transfer to a small bowl, cover and chill.

Drain the almonds, then put in a clean food processor with the dates and blend to a stiff paste, adding a little water if necessary. Take a generous tablespoon of the mixture and roll into a ball, then push the ball into a mini tart pan, pressing to line the edges. Repeat with the remaining mixture to line 6 mini tart tins. Chill for 20 minutes.

Remove the tart cases from the tins by running a knife around the edges. Spoon some of the cashew filling into each tart, then top with the raspberries. Drizzle over the remaining maple syrup and serve decorated with mint leaves.

For raspberry, almond & mango crumble, place 175 g (6 oz) chopped ready-to-eat dried apricots and the grated rind and juice of 1 orange in a bowl and leave to soak for 1 hour. Place 1 large peeled, stoned and chopped mango in a shallow ovenproof dish and pour over the apricots and juice, then scatter over 150 g (5 oz) raspberries. Sprinkle over 75 g (3oz) ground almonds, then pour over 25 g (1 oz) melted coconut oil. Bake in a preheated oven, 200°C (400°F), Gas Mark 6, for 15 minutes until lightly golden. Divide between 6 bowls and serve immediately. **Calories per serving 206**

index

acknowledgements

Senior Commissioning Editor Eleanor Maxfield
Project Editor Clare Churly
Design and Art Direction Penny Stock
Special Photography William Shaw
Food Stylist Joy Skipper
Prop Stylist Kim Sullivan
Picture Library Manager Jennifer Veall
Production Controller Sarah Kramer

Special photography © Octopus Publishing Group Limited/William Shaw. **Additional photography** © Octopus Publishing Group/Will Heap 23, 33, 63, 97, 117, 139, 177, 187, 233; David Munns 41, 85, 103, 151, 159, 193, 197, 207, 219, 223; Sean Myers 125, 203; Lis Parsons 15, 45, 51, 55, 127, 161, 175, 191, 215, 229, 231; William Reavell 165; Craig Robertson 201; Gareth Sambidge 155; William Shaw 13, 27, 57, 61, 71, 73, 75, 81, 89, 93, 107, 123, 131, 133, 137, 145, 167, 209, 213, 217, 225.